# Diving Deep and Surfacing

# Diving Deep and Surfacing

## Women Writers on Spiritual Quest

**Third Edition**
*With a new Afterword*

**Carol P. Christ**

Beacon Press
Boston

Beacon Press
25 Beacon Street
Boston, Massachusetts 02108-2892

Beacon Press books are published under the auspices
of the Unitarian Universalist Association
of Congregations in North America.

*Library of Congress Cataloging-in-Publication Data*

Christ, Carol P.
  Diving deep and surfacing : women writers on spiritual quest /
Carol P. Christ—with a new afterword.
    p.    cm.
  Originally published: 2nd ed. 1986.
  Includes bibliographical references and index.
  ISBN 0-8070-6207-3
  1. Women and religion.  2. Spiritual life.  I. Title.
  BL458.C47  1995
  291.4'082—dc20        95-22312

Grateful acknowledgment is made for permission to quote from the following:
*Surfacing* by Margaret Atwood, Copyright © 1972 by Margaret Atwood, Reprinted by permission of Simon & Schuster, a Division of Gulf & Western Corporation; *The Four-Gated City* by Doris Lessing, Copyright © 1969 by Doris Lessing, Reprinted by permission of Alfred A. Knopf, Inc.; *Diving into the Wreck* and *A Dream of a Common Language* by Adrienne Rich, Copyright © 1973 and 1978, respectively, by Adrienne Rich, Reprinted by permission of W. W. Norton & Company, Inc.; *for colored girls who have considered suicide / when the rainbow is enuf* by Ntozake Shange, Copyright © 1975, 1976, 1977 by Ntozake Shange, Reprinted with permission of Macmillan Publishing Co., Inc.; "Fight Back" by Holly Near from *Imagine My Surprise*, Copyright © 1978 by Hereford Music, Recorded on Redwood Records, 1978, Ukiah, California, All rights reserved/used by permission; "Old Time Woman," lyrics by Jeffrey Langley and Holly Near, music by Jeffrey Langley, Copyright © 1973 by Hereford Music, "Water Come Down," lyrics by Holly Near, music by Jeffrey Langley, Copyright © 1973 by Hereford Music, Both songs from *Holly Near: A Live Album*, Redwood Records, 1974, Ukiah, California, All rights reserved/used by permission; "Scars" by Meg Christian from *I Know You Know*, Copyright © 1974, Recorded on Olivia Records, Los Angeles, California, All rights reserved/used by permission; "Wild Things," "Song of the Soul," "Waterfall," and "Sister" by Cris Williamson from *The Changer and the Changed*, Copyright © 1975 by Bird Ankles Music, BMI, Recorded on Olivia Records, 1975, Los Angeles, California, All rights reserved/used by permission.

To my grandmothers

Mary Rita Inglis Christ
1898–1960

and

Lena Marie Searing Bergman
1891–1970

whose sense of the mysteries of life
inspired my spiritual quest

And to my two friends and colleagues

Judith Plaskow

and

Naomi Goldenberg

who have supported my work on this book
and whose thinking has become
intertwined with mine over
many years of work together

# Contents

# Preface to the Second Edition

IN *The Flight of the Seventh Moon*[1] the Native American shaman Agnes Whistling Elk teaches Lynn Andrews a ritual of giveaway in which she ties a copy of Andrews' book *Medicine Woman* to a tree with ribbons, leaving it there for a passer-by to take. In this way Lynn Andrews learns that her book is not hers, that it has come through her, but must find its own way in the world. In the years since I finished *Diving Deep and Surfacing,* I have learned that it too has found its own way. Wherever I speak, I am profoundly touched by women and men who tell me that *Diving Deep* has changed their lives. When this happens I am reminded that I am not alone. I am profoundly renewed and inspired with a sense of responsibility as I learn that I, like the authors I wrote about, was able to articulate something others were feeling too. In Tilburg, the Netherlands, I was asked to meet with a class of twenty women at the Theological University who were using *Diving Deep* as their major resource. As I listened to a tall, strapping young theological student present the class's questions to me in flawless, Dutch-accented English, I felt the "dream of a common language" coming into being.

I now feel an enormous distance from the young woman in her twenties who first began late at night in Montreal in June 1973 to name her thoughts about prophetic vision and women's spiritual quest in Doris Lessing's *The Four-Gated City*. I have a vivid image of her sitting on the floor long after midnight, sorting sheaves of yellow notebook paper with quotes and ideas written on them into piles, trying to bring order to the many insights and feelings she had had during the previous years when Lessing's work was one of her few anchors in a sea of patriarchal writing about religion. That young woman lived in a very different universe than I do now, a world in which *Beyond God the Father* and other classic works in feminist theology had not yet been published. Though she had the constant support of her friend and sister feminist theologian Judith Plaskow, she felt very alone and often wondered if there was anyone besides her friend Judith who could understand the vision, the experience, she was trying to name. Somehow she held tight to her intuition, validated in the words of Lessing, that if she was feeling something deeply in that growing place within herself, then others must be feeling it too, because others are products of the same times, the same historical and cultural forces. Though she knew this to be true at some level of her being, she continually doubted herself and her ideas. All around her the voices of patriarchy were "throbbing at [her] ears like midges, [telling her] nothing, nothing of origins, nothing [she] needed to know, nothing that could re-member [her]."[2] I admire her bravery forged in ignorance of the enormity of the task she was undertaking and of the support she would receive from other women as she named her experiences, insights, and visions. I feel for the nothingness and isolation she knew. Sometimes I am amazed that any of us survived those times to speak new language. And then I remember that sisterhood is indeed powerful. Without my friends, my students, my colleagues in the Women and Religion section of the American Academy of Religion and in the New York Feminist Scholars in Religion, I would never have been able to write *Diving Deep*.

One of the conflicts I felt in writing *Diving Deep* had to do with voice. Every word of my book was forged in the crucible of personal experience and struggle. And yet everything in my training told me that I had to present my work in an impersonal, dispassionate, third-person "objective" "scholarly" voice. I desperately wanted my work to be accepted by other scholars, by male scholars who hold the power in my field, because I wanted to find my way back into graduate teaching in Religious Studies, where I felt I could have the most impact on the future of feminist studies in religion. But I also wanted to be true to my own experience and to write in a way that would be understood by many other women.

This conflict highlights a significant methodological issue in the field of feminist studies. Many feminist scholars recognize that academic writing is often unnecessarily opaque and inaccessible. Because we feel an obligation to the community out of which our scholarship has emerged, we try to write in a way that is both scholarly and comprehensible to the nonspecialist. This sometimes means that our work is unfairly dismissed as being unscholarly. Even more critical, and more deeply challenging to the scholarly ethos, is our recognition that "objectivity" is a myth. We understand that even the most seemingly objective scholarship in every field reflects an implicit interest in preserving the patriarchal status quo, including certain notions of canon, authority, and tradition from which the contributions of women and others have been excluded. However, because these concerns are usually unstated, they often go unrecognized. But when feminist scholars discuss the interests which inspire our work, such as understanding our own lives and the lives of other women and transforming scholarship and the social world in which it is embedded, our work is often dismissed as being merely personal or polemical. Until the scholarly ethos is transformed, our work will appear anomolous within it. The transformation of the ethos of scholarship is one of the most serious tasks we face as feminist scholars.[3]

In *Diving Deep*, I made the uneasy compromise of relegating the personal experience which inspired my work to the preface and writing the rest of the book in a voice which was third person, but not dispassionate. If I were writing *Diving Deep* now, I would change all the references to women and "their" experiences to women and "our" experiences and I would write more directly about my own life, rather than disguising it with phrases like "a woman feels . . ." In my current writing, I am seeking to find a voice and a style of writing that is passionate, personal, political *and* scholarly, and reflective. I also regret that I did not insist that the methodological reflections in my article "Feminist Studies in Religion and Literature,''[4] which my editor rightly recognized was written in a dispassionate voice not compatible with the rest of my manuscript, be included as an appendix to *Diving Deep*. But I know that the reader of *Diving Deep* connects to both its passion and its scholarship.

*Diving Deep* was written at a time when most white feminist theorists were using the term ''women's experience'' uncritically. Though our sources for the most part reflected white, North American or European, twentieth-century middle-class women's experiences, we wrote as if women's experiences were undifferentiated and universal. In the intervening years, feminist theorists who are not white—North American or European—and middle class have criticized the false universalism implicit in much of the feminist theory developed by white feminists. Though I discussed the work of one nonwhite middle-class North American writer in *Diving Deep*, I was not as sensitive then as I am now to the need to consider the differences as well as the similarities of women's experiences across racial, class, ethnic, and national boundaries. If I were writing *Diving Deep* now, I would be less global in generalizing about women's experiences and I would not feel the need to justify the inclusion of lesbian and Black women's experiences to the white heterosexual reader.

In writing *Diving Deep* I also had to struggle to find a language with which to discuss women's spiritual quest. When I first read Doris Lessing's *The Four-Gated City*, I knew that what it evoked in me was ''spiritual,'' but I was not sure how to talk about it. I was certain that I didn't want to impose Christian categories of sin and grace on Martha's quest. But I didn't have a new language, a new vocabulary with which to articulate my sense of the book. I wanted to talk about the connection to larger powers Martha experienced in nature, through sexuality, with Lynda, and alone in her room. I finally adopted terms from mystical traditions, including ''nothingness,'' ''awakening,'' ''insight,'' and the word ''mysticism'' itself. I had to do this in order to make my intuitions comprehensible to others and to clarify them for myself. Yet I was also aware that the experiences portrayed by Lessing, Chopin, Atwood, Rich, and Shange were not ''classical'' mystical experiences as defined by Eastern or Western mystical traditions.

For example, "mystical" experiences in nature were generally dismissed by theorists and practitioners of mysticism as lower forms, stages on the way to a higher vision.[5] When I discussed nature mysticism in *Diving Deep*, I argued that it was not necessarily a lower form of mysticism. I only hinted at the conviction that has been growing in me since that time, that so-called "higher" mysticism represents a flight from the real conditions of our lives. Now I understand more clearly than I did then (in part because other women have been thinking similar thoughts) that ideas about higher and lower mysticism are a legacy of a type of dualistic thinking which, I am now prepared to argue, feminist spirituality and feminist thealogy call upon us to reject. This dualism has been named "absolute hierarchal dualism" by Mara Keller[6] in order to distinguish it from thinking in dualities, which need not be a negative feature of thought. In absolute hierarchal dualism it is said that there is a world beyond this world which is unchanging and infinite and therefore superior to this world of finitude and change. Plato argued in *The Symposium* that *eros* moves us from love of beautiful bodies and all that is changeable to a vision of the "Good" that is unchanging, unaffected by all that comes into being and passes away.[7] Many religious thinkers have identified Plato's vision of the Good with the mystical vision of God. All the terms of the mystical vocabulary are thus tinged with flight from the finite. For many who hear them, words like "nothingness," "awakening," "insight," and "mysticism" imply the Platonic or Platonic-Christian journey of the soul away from the pleasures of this world toward union with an unchanging transcendent source.

When I used terms from the mystical tradition, I was engaging in what deconstructionists call "deformation of language." I used traditional language, but in a context which gave it a different meaning. For example, in discussing nothingness in women's experience, I was pointing to something that is talked about in mystical traditions, namely a powerful experience of finitude or limitation in which social structures and structures of consciousness which had provided meaning in a person's life are called into question and recognized as less than absolute. I argued that such experiences could give women the power to challenge patriarchal social structures and structures of consciousness which have defined us and kept us in subordinate positions.

I believed then, and I believe now, that finitude and limitation are rooted in the structure of our lives. There is no permanence in our finite lives, there are no absolutes, there is no one person or thing we can count on to provide meaning in our lives as we move through time and change. As I have written,[8] I believe that women's spiritual quest and feminist thealogy are drawing all of us, women and men, to accept finitude and change, to live in and through it, without trying to escape it. Thus the "deformation" of mystical language I was and am proposing is that we give up the quest to ally ourselves with a transcendent source or power which is beyond change, which is unaffected by that which comes into being and dies. For me the goal of the "mystical" quest is to understand that we are part of a world which is constantly transforming and changing.

If there is no unchanging source or principle or God with which the mind or soul can ally itself, then there is no "transcendence" in the classical sense. This does not mean that there is only pure immediacy. There is still room for awareness of and reflection on self and world. "Mystical" experiences within the finite and changing world would be moments when we are aware that we are part of a community, a history, or the natural world which is larger than ourselves, yet still subject to change. Awareness that this larger whole is still subject to death does not mean that we must therefore seek to distance ourselves radically from or escape from it. Nor does it mean that we should overemphasize the death aspects of our world. All that is subject to death is teeming with vibrant life as we are. It is also true, as Margaret Atwood eloquently stated, that "nothing has died, everything is alive, everything is waiting to become alive."[9]

To use language with awareness that we are de-forming it, deliberately changing its meaning by changing its context, is an exercise fraught with danger. We may be misunderstood by those with whom we agree because they do not understand the new contexts in which we use old words. Or we may evoke agreement from those with whom we disagree, because they too have not understood the new context which de-forms, re-forms, and trans-forms the meanings of the words we use. But this is the risk we take in attempting to make ourselves understood. Perhaps there is no other way to create new language.

My visit to the women and religion class in Tilburg inspired an innovative method of teaching *Diving Deep* that validates the new naming I attempted in the book. The Dutch women told me that during the first four weeks of their class, they used *Diving Deep* as a catalyst for the telling of their own stories, focusing each week on one of the moments of women's quest I had named: nothingness, awakening, insight, naming. They said that the sharing they had done was powerful. I was delighted and astonished, for the idea of sharing our experiences in relation to my book had not occurred to me. Since I was on my way to teach Women's Spiritual Quest at the Aegean (now International) Women's Studies Institute[10] in Míthimna, on the island of Lesbos, I quickly modified my teaching plans for the summer, incorporating the Dutch women's ideas into the class I had planned.

The process of remembering, sharing, healing, naming, and creating rituals that occurred in this class and others modeled on it which I have taught at subsequent sessions of the Institute and at the Pacific School of Religion has been deeper and more transformative for me and for the other women in the class than I could have imagined. In retrospect, I see that these classes themselves have become a ritual of initiation into women's spiritual quest. I share the process that has developed in some detail here not only because it validates the insights of *Diving Deep,* but also in hopes that other women will be inspired to share in it.

In Míthimna I teach *Diving Deep* in conjunction with *The Goddess*[11] by Christine Downing and *The Dream of a Common Language*[12] by Adrienne Rich; sometimes I also use *The Homeric Hymns*[13] and Charlene Spretnak's *Lost Goddesses of Early Greece.*[14] At the Pacific School of Religion, I have used *Diving Deep* with *Womanspirit Rising*[15] and *The Dream of a Common Language.* For each class of three or so hours, I focus readings around one of the themes of my book: women's stories, women's quest, nothingness, awakening, insight, naming. Within each class, we spend some time on lecture and discussion about the readings. After we have developed the theme and everyone understands it, we spend twenty to thirty minutes writing in our journals about our own lives in relation to the themes we have discussed. After that, in groups of three and four, we spend about thirty minutes sharing what we have written. Then the whole group of fifteen to thirty women comes back together to reflect on what we have learned through our writing and sharing. During this discussion, I usually ask one or two women to share what they have written with the larger group.

The experience of writing in class in the presence of others seems to evoke deeper reflection and sharing than either writing at home and sharing in class or simply sharing in class. It is easier for those of us who are insecure about our writing to write in the presence of other women who are also writing. The limited time for writing seems to encourage us to dive immediately into our depths. I always speak of the importance of writing freely, without self-censorship or concern for grammar, spelling, or sentence structure. Each of us can edit out anything too private or painful when we share in the small group. However, I urge each woman to read directly from her journal in the small group. It seems to be easier for many of us to share deep feelings, insights, fears if we read what we have written rather than speak about it. Also, when we read from our journals, we often get positive feedback about the power of our writing and about our abilities to name our experiences in a way that is meaningful to others.

It is important that the small groups be limited to three or four. Three or four are enough to make connections with each other's experiences, but not so many that anyone's experience gets lost within the group. It seems to be easier to share deeply personal experiences with two or three others than with a larger group. Furthermore, with this number the sharing time can be limited to about thirty minutes. I let the groups form spontaneously to give those who want to get to know everyone the chance to move around and those who feel more comfortable continuing with one or more of the same people to do so. But if there are women in the class who already know each other's stories well, I encourage them to choose different groups. The power of this process has amazed me. Women who don't know each other begin to develop trust in each other, to dive deeper into their own experiences, to comfort and support one another.

Usually I begin the first class by discussing my ideas about women's stories and women's spiritual and social quests, as discussed in chapters one and two of *Diving Deep*. I speak of the power evoked in the telling and sharing of our stories. I define religion and spirituality in a way that enables women to recognize the spiritual in all areas of their lives, not simply in relation to the institutional church or synagogue. After voicing my ideas about story and religion, I encourage the women to share their own ideas about story, quest, and religion, to ask questions, and to share their own ideas about spirituality and religion. Then we each find a quiet place within ourselves where we can think and write about our own relation to religion and spirituality. First we try to remember our earliest spiritual or religious memories. Perhaps we remember a grandmother lighting a candle or praying; perhaps we think of Christmas or Passover. If a woman has no memories of anything spiritual or religious in her early life, she can write about how it felt to grow up without the influence of religion. I encourage each woman to write as concretely as possible, evoking the physical context, the sights, sounds, smells, of her memories. For the second part of this exercise, I ask each woman to think of and write about an experience that defines her mature attitude toward religion or spirituality. She may write about how she stopped going to church or synagogue, or about how she developed adult faith, or about spiritual experiences she has had outside the framework of institutional religion. Then we share each of these experiences in small groups. After sharing, we come back together to reflect upon what we have discovered about ourselves and others. I often encourage several women to read from their journals to the larger group. Through this process we learn that as we articulate our own experiences and insights, we have the power to "hear each other into speech."[16]

As the instructor, I play a mixed role, both writing and sharing my own experiences and keeping an eye on the dynamics of the group, watching for a group or an individual who has touched something painful and needs my attention to get through it. This is particularly important as we move to the theme of the second class, the experience of nothingness.

Because most women are on intimate and painful terms with nothingness and many easily fall back into its depths, it is important that the second class be orchestrated carefully and sensitively. There must be enough time not only to descend briefly into our own nothingness, but also to make the journey back. It is preferable that this class not precede a break in class meeting time, such as a weekend or a vacation. It is important that anyone who needs continued support within the class, from other class members, or from me as teacher, as she comes to terms with her own experiences of nothingness, find it.

For this class we review the discussion of nothingness in the second chapter of *Diving Deep* and we discuss the depiction of nothingness in my chapter on Ntozake Shange's *for colored girls*. Shange's poetry evokes the nothingness each of us has experienced at times in our lives. I remind the group that our experiences of nothingness are powerfully influenced by our positions as women in a patriarchal culture. I also talk about nothingness as a spiritual experience, a stripping away of the façade of conventional reality that allows us to confront our own depths and to see the world without illusion. Out of this experience can come renewal and healing, and, as Rich tells us, discovery of "new language" for naming the world:

> No one who survives to speak
> new language, has avoided this:
> the cutting-away of an old force that held her
> rooted to an old ground
> the pitch of utter loneliness
> where she herself and all creation
> seem equally dispersed, weightless, her being a cry
> to which no echo comes or can ever come.[17]

These words from Rich's poem "Transcendental Etude" powerfully evoke the isolation we feel during the process of stripping away and also invite us to learn to see our experiences of nothingness as occasions for insight. After sharing our ideas about nothingness, we again take twenty or thirty minutes to draw into ourselves and write about a time in our lives when we knew nothingness. I stress that no one needs to write about an experience that seems too painful, but I also stress that it can be very healing to think again about and gain power from our experiences of nothingness. Women in my classes take enormous risks. They have written about deep depressions and "breakdowns." One brave young woman shared for the first time that she had been molested. Another wrote about being raped. Each time we write about nothingness, several of us break into tears. More than once I have found myself holding a sobbing woman in my arms. I have been amazed at the ability of the women in my classes to heal each other through touch. We spontaneously re-create the ancient ritual of laying on of hands just as Shange's women did in *for colored girls*. There is little any of us have experienced that does not evoke chords of response in other women. As we listen, nurture, and support one another, we re-live and transform our pain.

For me the transformation of nothingness into insight is the most important part of this process. I have found Christine Downing's chapters "Beginning with Gaia" and especially "Persephone in Hades" helpful in articulating the relation of nothingness and insight. In "Beginning with Gaia," Downing reminds us that Gaia, Earth, is power of life and death: there is no life without death, no joy of connection without separation. She encourages us to see Demeter, Giver of grain, nurturer and sustainer of the upper world, and her daughter Persephone, Queen of the Underworld and death, as two aspects of the same whole. Both light and dark, seed and harvest, are holy. Downing writes that she once viewed Persephone primarily as victim, taken to the underworld against her will.[18] But she came to understand that Persephone as Queen of the Underworld symbolizes the underworld as a place of depth and transformation. I invite the women in the class to think of their own experiences of nothingness in relation to Persephone. "What would it mean," I ask them, "for you to become Queen of your particular underworld, the one you have just written about? What insights have you gained? How have you become stronger through experiencing nothingness?" We then take some time to meditate on ourselves as Queen of our own underworld and to write about what that could mean for us. Then we return to the same small groups with which we shared our experiences of nothingness and share our insights. When we come back together, we share the transformations we are beginning to experience. Again, several women usually agree to read parts of what they have written to the larger group. Each of us is strengthened by the sharing of our stories. Though sharing nothingness can be painful for many of us, it also enables the class to become a crucible for personal growth and transformation.

Awakening is the theme for the next class. We review the section of chapter two in *Diving Deep* on awakening and also discuss awakening as portrayed in my chapter on Kate Chopin's *The Awakening*. Chopin's words powerfully evoke the feelings of awakening:

> But the beginning of things, of a world especially is necessarily vague, tangled, chaotic, and exceedingly disturbing. How few of us emerge from such a beginning!
>
> . . . . . . . . . . . . . . . . . . . . . .
>
> She turned her face seaward to gather in an impression of space and solitude, which the vast expanse of water, meeting and melting with the moonlit sky, conveyed to her excited fancy.
>
> . . . . . . . . . . . . . . . . . . . . . . . . . . . . . . . . . . . .
>
> A feeling that was unfamiliar but very delicious came over her. She walked all through the house, from one room to another, as if inspecting it for the first time. . . . The flowers were like new acquaintances.[19]

If we are also reading Downing, we discuss her chapter on Aphrodite. Aphrodite and *The Awakening* go very well together. Aphrodite as Goddess of the sea and of transformation, especially sexual transformation, fits very well with the themes of Chopin's novel in which Edna's awakening is mediated by sensual experiences in the sea and with Robert. I speak of awakening as a time when the light begins to dawn, when we begin to see the world in a new way. We have all known many awakenings in our lives, sexual, spiritual, emotional, political. After we have discussed awakening in general terms, we turn again to our journals and write about a time in our lives when we experienced awakening in a powerful way. Most of us write of sexuality or the sea. Some of us come to see the connections between spirituality and sensuality, spirituality and sexuality, for the first time. Many of us speak of the difficulty of integrating experiences of deep intensity into our ordinary lives, a problem which Chopin's Edna was unable to resolve. Some of us have made pilgrimages to the temple of Aphrodite at Mesa not far from Míthimna to continue the process of integration begun in the class.[20]

The next theme is insight. For this class we review chapter two of *Diving Deep* and discuss Margaret Atwood's depiction of the process of coming to insight in *Surfacing*. Insight names moments of lucidity, when the meaning of our lives seems clear. Insight may come through mystical experiences in nature, as it did for Atwood's character; often it comes at times of crisis in our lives; sometimes it comes completely unexpectedly. If we are also reading Downing, we discuss her chapter on Artemis. Artemis as depicted by Downing is a Goddess who is powerfully alone, who chooses solitude in the wild places in nature. Like Atwood's unnamed protagonist, Artemis reminds us that we often come to insight while alone in nature, separated from the concerns of the city and mundane life. We read passages from Atwood's protagonist's journey:

> I am by myself; this is what I wanted, to stay here alone.
> . . . . . . . . . . . . . . . . . . . . . . . . . . . . . . . .
> The truth is here.
> . . . . . . . . . . .
> The earth rotates, holding my body down as it holds the moon;
> the sun pounds in the sky, red flames pulsing from it, searing
> away the wrong form that encases me.
> . . . . . . . . . . . . . . . . . . . . . . .
> I lean against a tree, I am a tree leaning . . .[21]

We speak of times in our lives when we sought or found healing solitude in nature, and of other times and places where we have gained insight. We discuss the fears and taboos or simply the lack of language that kept us from naming these times as times of insight, these experiences as spiritual. Again we write about and share our experiences of insight.

Our last session on naming gives us a final opportunity to articulate the insights we have gained through the process of individual and collective reflection on our lives, on our spiritual quests.

Often we precede this last session by reading and discussing Adrienne Rich's "Transcendental Etude," a poem touching on the themes of nothingness, awakening, insight, and naming. In this poem Rich names the power of women in her life, a power each of us has experienced, and been reminded of, through the sharing we have done together. After we write our own "namings" in our journals, we usually choose to share what we have written with the entire group. It is best if we simply go around the circle, with each woman reading what she has written without comment from the others. This way no one's experience and naming gets dissipated. By the end of our time together, we feel free enough with each other not to need the safety of the small group. Moreover, most of us want to hear the namings of each of the other women.

For the last class we create a group altar. Each woman contributes something that for her symbolizes her quest—a stone, a candle, a flower—anything. One woman brought a sandal, another a poem. The altars we create are always very beautiful. Creating altars is a very ancient woman's tradition and touches chords that are very deep in all of us.

The other part of our last class centers around the interpretation of Adrienne Rich's "Twenty-One Love Poems" as an example of a woman's spiritual quest. Rich's poems bring together the themes of women's quest, which we have been sharing in our class, and provide an example of the insight and integration we have sought through naming and sharing our experiences. Each woman reads and interprets the poem she had previously selected and studied, again without comment, addition, or criticism. The symphony of voices and diversity of interpretations reflects our unity and difference as women. Rich's poems always touch everyone in the class. Even those who initially resisted the interpretation of poetry, or who chose a poem because it was one of the only ones left, often report that it seems as if their poem chose them, because it articulates a dimension of their own lives and quest.

I have been amazed at the power of this process, at the depth women generate through the telling of our stories and reflecting on our spiritual quests. Through this process many women undergo dramatic spiritual and personal transformations and come to terms with difficult areas in their lives that might have taken years of therapy to resolve. Often some of the women create rituals that they perform separately, with a few others, or invite the group to share. One small group that had shared many tears in telling their stories of nothingness came to class the next day with a bowl and pitcher and invited us each to pour our own private suffering into the well of women's tears. They then blessed the water and sprinkled each of us with the renewal that comes through our sharing. Another time a woman who had shared the pain of being called by a ''cute'' ''diminutive'' name all her life invited us to share a ritual of literal new naming, in which she gave up her old name and took a new one. One year a woman who had been struggling to come to terms with her mother's death for twenty years of her life and several years of therapy finally was able to forgive her mother for dying. She asked several of us to share in a ritual where she laid her mother's soul to rest in the Greek land her mother had loved. During the ritual a beautiful blue butterfly, symbol of the soul to the ancient Greeks, fluttered around the spot. The young woman who had been molested created, with the help of several other women, a ritual in which she threw stones into the sea, naming her pain and violation: the burdens of shame, guilt, and anger she had been carrying alone for many years. She then set beautiful flowers adrift in the sea, naming with each one the power she was taking back into herself: her innocence, her youth, her sexuality, her beauty, her control over her body.

The power that we have gained and shared through this process evoked by naming, which has been done by women writers and by each of us as we share ''the truths which we are salvaging/from the splitting-open of our lives,''[22] confirms the insight I had when I began to write *Diving Deep*. The telling of women's stories and the naming of women's spiritual quest has the power to transform our lives and our relation to the world in which we live. The insights we have

gained are by no means final. We will continue to grow and change.
But our journey has begun. And we are strengthened by our growing
knowledge that we are not alone.

Carol P. Christ
*Míthimna and Berkeley, 1985*

# Preface

THOUGH THE IDEA for this book was conceived when I first read *The Four-Gated City,* its roots go back to my grandmothers. A summer spent with my Scotch-Irish Catholic grandmother, Mary Rita Inglis Christ, when I was six years old was probably the beginning of my sense of the mystery of life. I remember rising at dawn when it seemed we two were the only ones awake, going with her to early mass, learning to dip my fingers in holy water as we entered a still dark church, and rising and kneeling according to an unfamiliar rhythm. Candles flickering in deep red and blue glass and her pink rosary beads sparkling in shadowy light seemed to hold a secret I longed to understand. I also remember half listening to incredible stories of miraculous cures while playing on the living-room floor of my other grandmother, Lena Searing Bergman, a German-Scotch-English Christian Scientist. But for me her real magic was in her garden, fragrant with scents, alive with colors and textures—gardenias, roses, hibiscus, bluebelles—and, most marvelous of all, stately peacocks which flew over from the nearby arboretum. Hers was also the woman's magic of holiday dinners with the family gathered around tables laden with food and set with delicate china, glittering silver, and shimmering crystal. When she died and our parents sold her home, my brothers, cousins, and I felt we had lost our connection to an essential source of power.

I gained another intuition of great power from the ocean. As a young girl I spent long summer days at the beach, blissfully curling my toes in the sand, licking salt from my lips, attuning my body to the rhythms and currents of the waves, refusing to come out of the water even when my knees turned blue. As a teen-ager floating on my back out beyond the breakers, I remember thinking I was perfectly happy and could die at that moment without regret. Once when I was eighteen my eight-year-old brother and I were playing in the heavy surf on a deserted beach in early September. Unaware of a swift under-tow, we were pulled out over our heads. Unable to gain a footing, I scooped my little brother into my arms, threw him with all my power toward shore, and a wave carried him in. As I fought to swim to shore the waves crashed faster and faster over my head; there wasn't time between breakers to catch my breath. Thinking I would die, I said a last prayer, stopped struggling, and felt my body carried to shore. I cannot remember a time when I have not known in my bones that the sea is a great power. And though now I am more cautious, I still feel a sense of elation and peace at the beach.

Though this book is about women's experience, I lived twenty-two years as a woman before I consciously realized that women's experience is a problem. As a girl I read voraciously, and, never having been told what to read (great books being scarcely known in the schools I attended), I naturally sought out books about women. After graduating from Nancy Drew and *Double Date,* I moved on to *Gone with the Wind, Saratoga Trunk,* and a host of romantic stories about women, most of which I cannot remember today. When I arrived at college, I entered a world of books that was quite foreign to me. While my roommates had read Plato and Aristotle in high school, I didn't know whether the Golden Age of Greece was before or after the Middle Ages (which I thought were called the Dark Ages). I had no context for anything I was learning, but I had an enormous desire to enter this new world of books, because I hoped I might fit into it better than I had fit into the world of cheerleaders, football players, and dates. Moreover, these books were about questions of freedom, truth, and value, which had always interested me. I plunged myself into Nietzsche, Shakespeare, Conrad, and Aeschylus, not always fully understanding what they wrote, but entranced by their ideas.

Four years later, when I began graduate study in Religious Studies at Yale, I began to realize that I was an anomaly in a man's world. Certainly my experience was intensified because Religious Studies was populated almost entirely by men and because Yale, while it admitted a few women on the graduate level, was still guarding its centuries-long tradition as a gentleman's school. During my years there, Yale's president was to make the infamous statement that Yale would never admit women as undergraduates because its mission was to educate 1000 male leaders each year. But I had not expected this experience. I had come to study truth, and truth was no respecter of gender, I thought. That I was one of the two women (out of close to 100 students) in my graduate program should make no difference. To my surprise I learned that it made a great deal of difference. My colleagues and professors saw me as charming, and though they were delighted to have a young woman around, few seemed to expect I would complete my studies. My comments in classes were often ignored, and when I talked about my favorite theologian, Martin Buber, I was told he was a "poet," not a theologian. Buber's notion that a person could have an I–Thou relationship with a tree, an idea I used to interpret my experiences in the ocean, was singled out as an example of what was disparagingly called the "confusion" in his thought.

Gradually I began to wonder whether I had a different perspective on theology because I was a woman. When I talked about the spiritual experiences that gave rise to my interest in theology—my connection to nature, the oneness with the universe I had experienced while swimming in the ocean or hiking in the woods—I was told that such experiences were "aesthetic," "poetic," "emotional," or "confused" and not worthy of theological consideration. It began to seem crucially relevant to my situation that theologians had been men. If theology were written from a male perspective and my perspective was female, that might explain why my professors and student colleagues—all but one of them male—often failed to understand my perspective on theological issues.

I began to search the libraries for religious and theological texts written by women that would verify my spiritual experience. Though I found the works of Simone Weil, Teresa of Avila, and a few others, I was not satisfied. I needed to find the story of a woman of my own time whose experience was more like my own. And I also began to wonder whether the minds of the few women who had written on religious subjects in the past had been constricted by prevailing theological or philosophical ideologies. Had they been able to express the full dimensions of their spiritual experience, or only those elements that fit into categories created by men? I wanted to know what women's religious experience would be like when it was articulated in women's own language, not forced into the structures of male theology.

When I first read *The Four-Gated City* in the winter of 1969, I knew I had found the text I was looking for. Ideas and feelings I was struggling to put into words were expressed in Lessing's story of Martha Quest. My connection to *The Four-Gated City* was so deep that I dreamed about it for weeks. I recommended it to my friend Judith Plaskow, who by then was sharing my search for a theology reflecting women's experience. She confirmed my feeling that Lessing had powerfully articulated women's spiritual quest. *The Four-Gated City* became a kind of touchstone for us over the next five years. It was uncanny how ideas and relationships we had not noticed in earlier readings would suddenly take on meaning as we reached new stages in our quests. Whatever we were learning in our own lives, Lessing had already put into words.

Though I sensed that *The Four-Gated City* was an articulation of a woman's spiritual quest, I did not then have the vocabulary to articulate my intuitions. Receiving no encouragement from my professors when I mentioned doing a thesis on Doris Lessing using a religion and literature approach, I decided to write on Elie Wiesel instead. Knowing that I could not pursue my interests in women's religious experience without support from other women, I decided to organize a women's caucus at the 1971 meetings of the American Academy of Religion. Whereas in 1969 and 1970 I had seen no more than two or three other women at the annual meetings in my field, in 1971 there were at least forty of us, and we were visible. We nominated and elected Christine Downing to become president of the A.A.R., and, in order to share research, we established a "working group" on Women and Religion, which later was granted status as a regular section.

In 1973, at the second meeting of the Women and Religion working group, I presented my first paper on women's spiritual quest, "Explorations with Doris Lessing in Quest of the Four-Gated City," which is the basis of chapter five of this book. Writing that essay was difficult. Little had been published in the area of women and religion at that time, and there was no vocabulary for discussing women's spiritual quest. Luckily Judith Plaskow was just across town working on a similar project. In countless conversations, we checked and challenged each other's readings of Lessing and developed a vocabulary with which to name Lessing's articulation of women's experience.

Later that year, when I taught my first course on Women and Religion at Columbia, my students responded strongly to works by Lessing, Adrienne Rich, and Denise Levertov. They too sensed that in these works their own spiritual struggles were being depicted, not just talked about. Over the past several years I have taught courses on Women's Spiritual Quest at Pacific School of Religion, Columbia University, and San Jose State University. And I have found that whenever women read Kate Chopin, Margaret Atwood, Ntozake Shange, Lessing, Rich, and other women writers, a special feeling develops. Friendships are formed which extend beyond the classroom, and the women sense that something which will affect them deeply for years to come has begun to happen through our discussions.

During the years that I have been thinking about this book, themes and images from the novels and poems have reflected and validated my own spiritual quest. Martha Quest's mystical experiences in nature validated my own experiences and gave me strength to pursue my own insights. Kate Chopin's evocation of the power of the sea and Margaret Atwood's heroine's experiences in nature and the woods were also especially important to me.

Later, when I began to write about Lessing, I found that my best writing time was between midnight and dawn. Awake when the rest of the city slept, I created a space where I was free of all distractions and could begin to enter more deeply into Martha Quest's world and the world of my own insights. One night when I was thinking about how Martha "connected" to "currents and forces of energy," waited and let them "collect," I tuned into a powerful energy source. I found myself able to do push-ups, sit-ups, and other exercises that I had never been able to do. Staying up late, I often felt I reached that "clear lit space" of vision and insight Martha talked about.

I began to trust my own insights more and more as others responded positively to my teaching, lecturing, and writing about Lessing. I learned, as Martha also had learned, that when I expressed what I thought and felt when I was most deeply in touch with my inner self and most open to the world around me, I was not alone—others were thinking and feeling the same things.

Lessing's celebration of Martha's solitude as a place where insight can be gained was also an important image for me during the years I lived as a single woman in New Haven and New York. I began to view myself as a woman like Martha, whose strength came from her solitude, from confronting the darkness within and without and then coming through to the other side.

Adrienne Rich's poems in *Diving into the Wreck* also reflected my struggle. Like Rich, I had sensed that men's ability to remain "strong" and emotionally distant in relationships was part of the same warped patriarchal mentality that allowed them to retain emotional distance while discussing poverty in the ghetto or bombing in Vietnam. And, like Rich, I felt that far from being a sign of irrationality, women's emotionality and personal involvement is a positive, life-affirming value. I also sensed a spiritual import in Rich's metaphor of diving beneath the wreck of patriarchal civilization in search of a hidden treasure.

When I first read Margaret Atwood's *Surfacing,* I was struggling with images of myself as powerless and powerful. Because I had only negative patriarchal images of power, I was wary of power altogether. *Surfacing,* however, clarified my relationship to power. The heroine's understanding that her power stemmed from her clear understanding of her rooting in nature and in her own personal past provided me with an alternative notion of power as insight and grounding. Her protagonist's words, "this above all, to refuse to be a victim . . . to give up the old belief that I am powerless," seemed directed to me. For years I would quote them to myself as I struggled to accept the power that comes from being oneself and expressing one's perceptions of the world.

Ntozake Shange's depiction of women's self-destructive dependence on men was also important to me. When Naomi Goldenberg and I first saw Shange's play *for colored girls who have considered suicide/when the rainbow is enuf,* we both felt that we had been reborn in a small way as we witnessed the tall Black woman in red rise from the floor of the stage to affirm the source of power within and without her. Shange's boldness in naming "god in myself" seemed right to us, since we recently had begun together to speak the name "Goddess" and had felt this new naming as a powerful antidote to the self-abasing dependence on men that both of us, like Shange, had known too well.

I had wildly mixed feelings when I first read Adrienne Rich's new poems in *The Dream of a Common Language.* Her naming of the power of female vision and creativity in the "humdrum acts / of attention to this house / transplanting lilac stickers ... sweeping stairs, brushing the thread / of the spider aside" reminded me of the woman's mystery I had sensed in my grandmother's home and garden. I loved Rich's celebration of a solitude that can be chosen without loneliness. And I found her depiction of "a passivity we mistake / —in the desperation of our search— / for gentleness" an all-too-accurate description of the quality that had drawn me to a man I had loved too much. But I had trouble with Rich's vision of relationships. Perhaps because I have known solitude and living alone so deeply in my life, I found it hard to accept her view that "two people together is a work / heroic in its ordinariness." I find heroine-ism more in the years I and my women friends have lived alone than in relationships with women or men. And though I agree with Rich that learning to love women/ourselves could transform cultural values, I do not share her lesbian vision.

This book is the product of many years of thinking and struggle. To name everyone who has influenced it would be impossible. But I would especially like to thank Judith Plaskow, who has been a close friend and colleague for over a decade and with whom I have discussed every idea in this book and many others many times, and Naomi Goldenberg, a newer but equally good friend and sister who has shared so many of my academic and personal struggles over the past five years. Marcia Keller, Carolyn Forrey, and Caroline Whitbeck also deserve special mention as colleagues, critics, and friends. Celia Behrman Weisman came from New York during the summer of 1979 to work with me and her enthusiasm, insight, and hard work made it much easier for me to finish this book. In the years to come she too will be writing on women's quest. The brave and pioneering work of Valerie Saiving, Mary Daly, and Rosemary Ruether made this book and much else possible. The women in the New York Feminist Scholars in Religion, especially Anne Barstow, Karen Brown, Ellen Umansky, Beverly Harrison, Sheila Collins, Alice Carse, and Nelle Morton, and the Women's Caucus–Religious Studies, especially Christine Downing, Elisabeth Schüssler Fiorenza, and Rita Gross, have helped to create a context in which we all could think new thoughts. Ellen Boneparth, Selma Burkom, Sybil Weir, Fanny Rinn, Billie Jensen, Margaret Williams, Bettina Aptheker, Jo Stuart, and the other women in Women's Studies at San Jose State University have shown me that it is possible for academic women to support each other both in the university and outside it. Starhawk, Hallie Iglehart, and Z. Budapest taught courses that encouraged me to think more freely about women, nature, and Goddesses. Elizabeth Fishel's writing course helped me write more boldly. The students in my classes at Columbia, Pacific School of Religion, and San Jose State have provoked me to develop and sharpen my thinking about women's spiritual quest. Ellen Morgan, Catherine Stimpson, and Carolyn Heilbrun provided helpful comments and needed encouragement on early drafts of my essays on Lessing and Atwood. Patricia Parks, Gail Kong, Kit Havice, and Beverly Steckel have also shared my quest to understand women's experience. Janice Campisi, Ann Younger, and Dianne Lindsey typed the manuscript. Joanne Wyckoff at Beacon provided helpful editorial advice. Without these women and many others, this book would not have been written. Several men also deserve mention. Michael Novak, Stephen Crites, James E. Dittes, Julian N. Hartt, Wayne Proudfoot, Tom Driver, and Joseph L. Blau have encouraged my work through the years, often when others did not. Roger Robinson helped me create a home space in which the final draft of this book could be completed. The National Endowment for the Humanities provided a summer stipend in 1978, for which I am grateful.

# 1. Women's Stories, Women's Quest

WOMEN'S STORIES have not been told.* And without stories there is no articulation of experience. Without stories a woman is lost when she comes to make the important decisions of her life. She does not learn to value her struggles, to celebrate her strengths, to comprehend her pain. Without stories she cannot understand herself. Without stories she is alienated from those deeper experiences of self and world that have been called spiritual or religious. She is closed in silence. The expression of women's spiritual quest is integrally related to the telling of women's stories. If women's stories are not told, the depth of women's souls will not be known.

Stories give shape to lives. As people grow up, reach plateaus, or face crises, they often turn to stories to show them how to take the next step. Women often live out inauthentic stories provided by a culture they did not create. The story most commonly told to young girls is the romantic story of falling in love and living happily ever after. As they grow older some women seek to replace that story with one of free and independent womanhood. Doris Lessing's character Martha Quest was such a woman. When she wanted to know what to do with her life, Martha examined the lives of the two women she knew best, Mrs. Quest, her repressed and bitter mother, and Mrs. Van Rensberg, a fat Dutch farmwoman. Rejecting their lives as narrow and

*I will be using "story" in a broad sense to refer to all articulations of experience that have a narrative element, including fiction, poetry, song, autobiography, biography, and talking with friends.

constricting, Martha turned to fiction, hoping to find, "if not in literature, which evaded these problems, then in life, that woman . . . [who
was] a 'person.'"[1] Martha felt her life opening before her, but she
couldn't shape it out of nothing: she needed a story of another woman
whose life was rich and full to provide her with an image of what her
own life might be. Like many other women, Martha failed to find the
image of a free woman in the literature she read. Instead of creating a
new story for herself, Martha found herself half-consciously drifting
into roles in the conventional stories of her time. She became the
attractive young woman who dances with suitors until dawn, the war
bride, the pregnant wife, the young mother. Without her willing it,
her story began to resemble that of the mother she had rejected.[2]

Martha's experience calls attention to the importance of stories
in lives, something most people intuitively know. When meeting new
friends or lovers people reenact the ritual of telling stories. Why?
Because they sense that the meaning of their lives is revealed in the
stories they tell, in their perception of the forces they contended with,
in the choices they made, in their feelings about what they did or did
not do. In telling their stories people speak of parents, friends, lovers,
ecstasy, and death—of moments when life's meaning seemed clear, or
unfathomable. People reveal themselves in telling stories.

But stories also reveal the powers that provide orientation in
people's lives. When people talk about books or movies that touched
them, about people they have loved or wanted to emulate, they speak
of that elusive sense of meaning, power, and value that roots their
mundane stories in something deeper. This depth dimension of stories
is crucial, for without it lives would seem empty, meaningless.

The theories about story and religion developed by Michael
Novak, Stephen Crites, and others help to elucidate the depth dimension of stories. Both Crites and Novak have noted that stories are more
than a simple recounting of experience. According to Crites every
story has a "sacred" dimension, "not so much because gods are commonly celebrated in them, but because [a woman's] sense of self and
world is created through them . . . For these are stories that orient the
life of a people through time, their life-time, their individual and
corporate experience and their sense of style, to the great powers

that establish the reality of their world."[3] Michael Novak expressed the same idea when he wrote, "Not to have any story to live out is to experience nothingness: the primal formlessness of human life below the threshold of narrative structuring. Why become anything at all? Does anything make any difference? Why not simply die?"[4] Crites and Novak state that stories create a sense of self and world. Crites's notion that stories provide "orientation" to "great powers" is crucial. Stories with a sacred dimension point to a source of meaning that gives purpose to people's lives.

Certain religious stories provide orientation to sources of meaning. For the religious Jew, the story of God's giving of the law on Sinai gives a depth dimension to the simplest act, from preparing a kosher chicken to lighting the Sabbath candles. A depth dimension is given to everyday activities because the Jew understands her position as one of God's chosen people. Similarly, the Christian orients her life around the life and death of Jesus. If her firstborn daughter dies in infancy, she will mourn, but her sense of loss will be tempered by her faith that the death of her child is somehow taken up and given meaning by the story of the death and resurrection of Jesus Christ, which for her expresses the universe's secret meaning.

What is less obvious, especially to those who identify religion or sacrality primarily with the stories in the Bible, is that many stories have a sacred dimension. All stories do not orient a person to the God revealed at Sinai or Golgotha, but many stories provide orientation to what Crites calls the "great powers that establish the reality of their world."[5] These powers may not be named divinities and they need not speak out of whirlwinds for their presence to be felt. They may be identified by their function of providing orientation. They are the boundaries against which life is played out, the forces against which a person must contend, or the currents in whose rhythms she must learn to swim. They sometimes provide revelation when the self is at a loss—when she doesn't know where to turn. They may provide a sense of meaning and value which is more potent than that offered by conventional stories. They may ground a person in powers of being that enable her to challenge conventional values or expected roles.

Common to all stories with this "sacred" dimension is the importance given to the story by teller or hearer. It might seem that all sacred stories would have to be realistic and serious, but this is not so. The story might be of adventure if the teller thinks adventure is what life is all about, a love story if love makes life meaningful, a fantasy if fantasy is the only way to achieve transcendence. What is common to all these stories is not their genre but their function in providing orientation to life's flow. Indeed the same story may be sacred to one person but not to another. Classic myths that were revelatory to the ancient Greeks became simple adventure stories for Christians, while Biblical stories are not revelatory for post-Christians.

Through recognizing the crucial importance of stories to selves, the dilemma of women is revealed. Women live in a world where women's stories rarely have been told from their own perspectives. The stories celebrated in culture are told by men. Thus men have actively shaped their experiences of self and world, and their most profound stories orient them to what they perceive as the great powers of the universe. But since women have not told their own stories, they have not actively shaped their experiences of self and world nor named the great powers from their own perspectives.[6]

Of course women appear in the stories of men, but only in roles defined by men — usually mothers, wives, sisters, lovers, nurses, assistants, or whores. Stories of mothers and daughters, of women's friendship, of women working with women, of women's love for each other are rarely told. "Chloe liked Olivia," a simple statement about a woman's feeling for another woman, is, Virginia Woolf wrote in *A Room of One's Own*, a sentence that has rarely appeared in literature. Readers have known Chloe only in relation to Roger and Percival. They have never heard how Chloe felt about her mother, whether she liked her sister, what she thought about when she was alone, whether she ever contemplated her position in the universe. When women tell their stories, Woolf suggested, "Chloe liked Olivia" will become commonplace. Readers will know how Chloe felt when she got up in the morning, what she did when Roger and Percival were not around, how she felt about the world.[7]

In a very real sense, there is no experience without stories. There is a dialectic between stories and experience. Stories give shape to experience, experience gives rise to stories. At least this is how it is for those who have had the freedom to tell their own stories, to shape their lives in accord with their experience. But this has not usually been the case for women. Indeed there is a very real sense in which the seemingly paradoxical statement "Women have not experienced their own experience" is true.

Women have lived in the interstices between their own vaguely understood experience and the shapings given to experience by the stories of men. The dialectic between experience and shaping experience through storytelling has not been in women's hands. Instead of recognizing their own experiences, giving names to their feelings, and celebrating their perceptions of the world, women have often suppressed and denied them. When the stories a woman reads or hears do not validate what she feels or thinks, she is confused. She may wonder if her feelings are wrong. She may even deny to herself that she feels what she feels.

For example, a young woman may think that she does not want children because she would like to have a career. If she hears stories about women who have not had children and are happy with the lives they have chosen, as well as stories of women who have combined career and family, then her feelings about her career and her questions about whether she can combine career and children will have been validated. She will be able to recognize and articulate her experience and make decisions on the basis of it. If, on the other hand, there is no validation for her experience, no shared articulation, she will have a dilemma. She will ask herself whether there is something wrong with her if she doesn't want children. She may learn to suppress and deny— even to herself—that she has ever thought of not having children.

And what of her thoughts about career? If there are no stories of women who work outside the home, what will she do? She may with some incredible effort "slide herself sidewise"[8] into the stories of men. A young woman who wants to do something significant may decide to be like a male figure she has admired. This identification may work for a while, but if she starts thinking about home and family, she is left without an image that fits her experience. The male figure she admired could be heroic without giving up the possibility of having children. But what will she do? Will she drift into marriage and motherhood? Will she try to combine marriage and motherhood with a career? Whatever choice she makes, it will be difficult for her if her feelings and conflicts are not articulated in the stories she has heard. Her choice may be even further complicated if she has heard the stories that men tell about career women: that they are aggressive, unwomanly, castrating bitches. Upon hearing such stories many women begin to doubt and suppress their own thoughts of attaining power or contributing to the larger society.

As women become more aware of how much of their own experience they must suppress in order to fit themselves into the stories of men, their yearning for a literature of their own, in which women's stories are told from women's perspectives, grows. This is why the new literature—fiction and poetry—written by women who are aware of the gap between women's experience and men's stories is so important for women. What Ntozake Shange wrote in *for colored girls who have considered suicide/when the rainbow is enuf* expresses all women's desperate need for stories:

> sing a black girl's song
> bring her out
> to know herself
> to know you
> . . . sing her song of life
> she's been dead so long
> . . . sing the song of her possibilities
> sing a righteous gospel
> the makin of a melody
> let her be born
> let her be born. (4–5)

What Shange says of song applies equally to story: without articulation, the self perishes. Black women's place in the stories of white men's culture is even more truncated than white women's. Even in stories told by white women or Black men, Black women's unique voices are not heard. Shange's use of the imagery of death and rebirth underscores the urgency of all women's storytelling. Without stories there is a sense in which a woman is not alive. Continually trying to fit her possibilities into stories where her reality is not acknowledged, a woman experiences nothingness, and perhaps even contemplates suicide, as suggested in the title of Shange's work.

The consciousness-raising group, from which the current women's movement was born, can be seen as a ritualized setting in which women gather together to share their stories. In consciousness raising, women "hear each other into speech," as Nelle Morton says. Her phrase captures the dynamic in which the presence of other women who have had similar experiences makes it possible for women to say things they have never said before, to think thoughts they would have suppressed. As Morton says, there is a hearing that occurs before speech and "evokes a new speech."[9] In consciousness raising new stories are born, and women who hear and tell their stories are inspired to create new life possibilities for themselves and all women.

Adrienne Rich named the creative potential of women's storytelling when she wrote, "two women, eye to eye / measuring each other's spirit, each other's / limitless desire, / a whole new poetry beginning here."[10] The simple act of telling a woman's story from a woman's point of view is a revolutionary act: it never has been done before. A new language must be created to express women's experience and insight, new metaphors discovered, new themes considered.[11] Women writers who name the gap between men's stories about women and women's own perceptions of self and world are engaged in creating a new literary tradition. And just as consciousness raising is a storytelling ritual, so too are feminist literary readings ritual events. As women writers share their naming of experience, they forge connections to other women who hear their own unnamed longings voiced, their perceptions of the world and its powers given form.

This new literature created by women has both a spiritual and a social dimension. It reflects both women's struggles to create new ways of living in the world *and* a new naming of the great powers that provide orientation in the world. In order to call attention to the spiritual dimension of women's quest, which is sometimes overlooked in the urgency of the struggle for new social roles, I have made a distinction between the spiritual and social quests. In making this distinction, I do not intend to separate reality into the spiritual and the mundane, as has been typical in Western philosophy. Rather, I believe women's quest seeks a wholeness that unites the dualisms of spirit and body, rational and irrational, nature and freedom, spiritual and social, life and death, which have plagued Western consciousness. Neither do I wish to suggest that the spiritual and social quests cannot or need not be united in the life of a single woman. Indeed my own life and the lives of many other women I know reflect precisely the struggle to unite spiritual and social. I believe that women's spiritual and social quests are two dimensions of a single struggle and it is important for women to become aware of the ways in which spirituality can support and undergird women's quest for social equality.

Women's *social quest* concerns women's struggle to gain respect, equality, and freedom in society—in work, in politics, and in relationships with women, men, and children. In the social quest a woman begins in alienation from the human community and seeks new modes of relationship and action in society. She searches to find nonoppressive sexual relationships, new visions of mothering, creative work, equal rights as a citizen. Women's social quest includes, but is not limited to, the political as it is commonly defined to include law and government. It also includes the realm of personal relationships and the intermediate realm of work. Recent women's thinking recognizes the ways in which family, work, and political relationships are intertwined and mirror each other. Hence the phrase "the personal is the political" reflects women's new consciousness.[12]

Stories of frustrated middle-class housewives and mothers' struggles for liberation such as Anne R. Roiphe's *Up the Sandbox* or Alix K. Shulman's *Memoirs of an Ex-Prom Queen* are common examples of the social quest genre. Doris Lessing's *The Golden Notebook,* which concerns two women's struggles to create the life of "free women" in work, politics, and relationships, is also about the social quest.

Women's *spiritual quest* concerns a woman's awakening to the depths of her soul and her position in the universe.[13] A woman's spiritual quest includes moments of solitary contemplation, but it is strengthened by being shared. It involves asking basic questions: Who am I? Why am I here? What is my place in the universe? In answering these questions, a woman must listen to her own voice and come to terms with her own experience. She must break long-standing habits of seeking approval, of trying to please parents, lovers, husbands, friends, children, but never herself. In probing her experience and asking basic questions, a woman may begin to wonder whether she has ever chosen anything she has done. A woman in my first con- sciousness-raising group described how she mentally stripped her house of everything she had not chosen freely. Going through each object and relationship one by one, she was finally left in an empty room with white walls, six months pregnant, a one-year-old child in a crib. Even her marriage had been a way of pleasing her parents. In allowing herself to experience the nothingness in a life lived by meeting others' expectations, a woman gives up her reliance on conventional stories or roles that had once provided meaning in her life. Because she can no longer accept conventional answers to her questions, she opens herself to the radically new—possibly to the revelation of powers or forces of being larger than herself that can ground her in a new understanding of herself and her position in the world.

The quest motif, which has a long history in Western literature, appears in different form in the new literature written by women. The quests of heroes, from Gilgamesh and Odysseus, Apuleius and Augus- tine, to Stephen Daedalus and Carlos Castaneda, have been recorded throughout history. Joseph Campbell in his classic work *The Hero with a Thousand Faces* charted the journey of the hero in many cultures. Typically the hero leaves home, defines himself through tests and trials, and returns with a clearer understanding of himself and his place in the world.[14] But if the hero has a thousand faces, the heroine has scarcely a dozen. Yet as Annis Pratt has noted, "if there is a 'myth of the hero' there must also be a 'myth of the heroine,' a female as well as a male *bildungsroman*, parallel perhaps, but by no means iden- tical."[15] Because female social roles are different from men's, the content of the female quest differs from that of the male.

Women's spiritual quest explores that dimension of stories which Crites called sacred, "not so much because gods are commonly celebrated in them, but because [a woman's] sense of self and world is created through them." They "orient the life of a people . . . to great powers that establish the reality of their world."[16] The nature of the "great powers" referred to by Crites, or, as I call them, "powers or forces of being larger than the self," cannot be defined other than functionally because they vary from story to story. In one story the "great powers" may be revealed through natural forces, in another through community or sisterhood. Crites's term is not intended to delineate or define the nature of the great powers—or even to say whether they are one power or many powers—but only to call attention to the way in which great powers provide orientation in stories. Deliberately more ambiguous than the terms "God" or "gods," "great powers" names the self's sense that it is related to something larger. Paul Tillich expressed a similar notion when he said that every individual derives "power of being" from the "ground of being" or "being itself." Without entering into disputes about what Tillich meant by being, it is still possible to see the aptness of Tillich's metaphor of "grounding." "Grounding" expresses the notion that the self is not only oriented to great powers, but is also supported by them just as the ground provides a place on which to stand.[17]

As I see it, the powers of being that orient and ground women's quest are best understood as "forces or currents of energy," to use Doris Lessing's term, which operate in all natural and social processes. These forces are the energies of life, death, and regeneration and being, nonbeing, and transformation, which are most obvious in nature, but which also operate in the social world. These forces are not only life forces, but forces of death and destruction. In nature the life and death forces are intertwined. Every individual is finite and eventually must die, but life also re-creates itself from death. The dead heron, which in Margaret Atwood's *Surfacing* provides food for swarms of insects that devour its flesh, is a graphic symbol of death transforming into life. It is not individuals, but the process of life transforming into death into life that is eternal—or seems so from a human perspective. The individual can gain a sense of transcendence from recognizing participation in these larger life and death forces.[18]

It is important for women to name the great powers or powers of being (I will use these two terms interchangeably) from their own perspective and to recognize their participation in them. Women need to recognize that their participation in the life and death forces in all natural processes means that they have as much right to exist and to affirm their value as every other being. Women also need to name their movement for greater equality as a movement rooted in the powers of being and life.[19]

Women's spiritual quest provides orientation for women's social quest and grounds it in something larger than individual or even collective achievements. As women begin to name their own experience and to name the world, they sometimes feel that all of history, all of nature, and even the gods are against them. Most of history has been told from the perspective of men's power. Research on biological differences between the sexes has been geared toward explaining men's dominance in society. And divinities in both Eastern and Western religions have been used to justify male superiority in family, society, and religion. While women's quest to overturn these ancient patterns can sometimes be supported by sheer inner determination, at other times the forces ranged against women's social quest seem overpowering. At this point a woman's spiritual quest can support her social quest. If a woman has experienced the grounding of her quest in powers of being that are larger than her own personal will, this knowledge can support her when her own personal determination falters.

It would, however, be a mistake to view women's spiritual quest simply as insurance against being overpowered by despair in the social quest. Women's spiritual quest undergirds every moment of women's social quest. A woman's recognition of the grounding of her social quest and that of other women in the powers of being which she has experienced gives her day-to-day confidence. Knowing that she has a right to her own mode of being can give her strength to stand up for her principles in a meeting, to create something beautiful in her craft, or to ask a friend, lover, or child to treat her as a person whose feelings and insights are as deep and as valuable as every other person's.

Moreover, women's spiritual quest involves a probing to the bedrock of a woman's experience of self and world that can support her quest to change the values of her society. Many women seek new visions of power and personhood and do not wish simply to become like men in their struggle for equality and justice. But it is sometimes difficult to see how power will be different when women have it. Women's spiritual quest is concerned with naming those differences.

The new stories that women tell each other in conversations with each other, in consciousness raising, and in fiction, poetry, and other literary forms are key sources for discovering the shape of women's spiritual quest. Indeed, as Naomi Goldenberg has said, fiction and poetry written by women may come to be viewed as "sacred texts" of a new spiritual consciousness.[20] Though this statement may seem odd to those who have studied women's writing from other perspectives, or to those whose studies of sacred texts have focused on canonized scriptures, it is a logical development of the perspective on women's stories and women's quest that I will be developing in this book. This does not mean necessarily that women writers deliberately set out to create new sacred texts.[21] What it does mean is that the telling of women's stories involves a new naming of the great powers and hence a new naming of the whole of women's experiences.

# 2. Nothingness, Awakening, Insight, New Naming

WOMEN'S SPIRITUAL QUEST takes a distinctive form in the fiction and poetry of women writers.[1] It begins in an *experience of nothingness*. Women experience emptiness in their own lives—in self-hatred, in self-negation, and in being a victim; in relationships with men; and in the values that have shaped their lives. Experiencing nothingness, women reject conventional solutions and question the meaning of their lives, thus opening themselves to the revelation of deeper sources of power and value. The experience of nothingness often precedes an *awakening*, similar to a conversion experience, in which the powers of being are revealed. A woman's awakening to great powers grounds her in a new sense of self and a new orientation in the world. Through awakening to new powers, women overcome self-negation and self-hatred and refuse to be victims.

Awakening often occurs through *mystical identification*, which women's traditional attunement to the body and mothering processes have prepared them for. Women's mystical experiences often occur in nature or in community with other women. Awakening is followed by a *new naming* of self and reality that articulates the new orientation to self and world achieved through experiencing the powers of being. Women's new naming of self and world often reflects wholeness, a movement toward overcoming the dualisms of self and world, body and soul, nature and spirit, rational and emotional, which have plagued

13

Western consciousness. Women's new naming of self and world suggests directions for social change and looks forward to the realization of spiritual insight in social reality—the integration of spiritual and social quests.

Though a woman's spiritual quest may proceed linearly from the experience of nothingness, through awakening, to mystical insight, and new naming, this order is not necessary. Sometimes awakening precedes awareness of the experience of nothingness, and mystical insight can intensify a woman's experience of the nothingness of conventional reality. It should not be assumed that a woman can ever be through with the experience of nothingness. As long as she lives—and especially in a male-centered society—the experience of nothingness will reappear. The moments of women's quest are part of a process in which experiences of nothingness, awakenings, insights, and namings form a spiral of ever-deepening but never final understanding.[2]

The *experience of nothingness* in women's spiritual quest has analogies to the dark night described in classical mystical texts. In *The Experience of Nothingness* Michael Novak pointed out the contemporary relevance of the mystical perception of the world. For him the mystic's notion of the "dark night of the soul" provided a useful paradigm for understanding the spirit of social unrest and protest that inspired the American civil rights, antiwar, and counterculture movements of the 1960s. The experience of the dark night of the soul is well expressed in the mystic's epigram, *"if you desire to possess everything, desire to have nothing."*[3] For the mystic, the dark night of the soul is a period of purgation in which all ties with the conventional world are broken in anticipation of revelation and union with a higher source of being and value. The "dark night" is a metaphor for the sense of emptiness felt by those who have broken their ties with conventional sources of value, but have not yet discovered their grounding in new sources. Novak felt that the experience of nothingness did not have to be feared if it could be seen as a stage in a journey toward greater insight. He argued that the experience of nothingness is not paralyzing—it is liberating. In its dark light, nothing is beyond questioning, sacred, immobile." Nonetheless, he believed that the "experience of nothingness may be absorbed in full sanity; that a clear and troubling recognition of our fragility, our mortality, and our ignorance need not subvert our relation to the world in which we find ourselves."[4] He felt that familiarity with the experience of nothingness was a good antidote to political naiveté and shallow idealism.

Though Michael Novak did not consider the sense of emptiness women feel as they realize their position in a world where women's experience is not valued, his notions provide a powerful paradigm for naming women's experience. Mary Daly recognized this first in her review of *The Experience of Nothingness*[5] and later in her book *Beyond God the Father*, where the experience of nothingness is a central category in her analysis of women's quest. Every human being is vulnerable to the experience of nothingness if each is willing to recognize what Novak calls "the formlessness, the aimlessness, and the disunity implicit in [one's] own insignificance, [one's] mortality, [one's] ultimate dissolution."[6] And while women share in the general human experience of finitude, women's experience of nothingness is more far reaching than men's. Women's experiences of nothingness begin at birth and continue throughout their lives. At a very young age a girl realizes that being female means understanding that her brothers have a right to demand more of their mother's attention, that her father will not play ball with her. Being female means that even if she gets A's, her career will not be as important as that of a boy who gets B's. Being female means that *she* is not important, except in her relationships to boys and men. Being female also means being given ambivalent messages. Parents and teachers rarely will tell a girl that she is less important than her brothers and other boys, for that would contradict the American ideal of equality and justice for all. The message of her inferiority will be communicated in more subtle ways: by lack of concern, by failure to fully nurture her potential for growth and development, by not expecting her to succeed at difficult tasks. And because the messages are mixed, a woman may feel that her mother's, father's, or teachers' lack of attention to her stems from some specific failing of her own. Internalizing the voices of her oppressors, the currents of her feelings of inferiority and self-hatred run strong and deep.

Women thus learn to doubt the value of their thoughts, their feelings, their creativity. They concede that the things women do are not valuable. They agree that making a home, rearing children, or being a nurse, secretary, or teacher are jobs requiring little creativity or skill—anyone can do them. And they believe that men's work, whether it is fixing cars, working on a factory line, building a house, or running a business, is more important than what women do. If they dare to challenge conventional patterns, they learn sooner or later that a woman's intelligence, creativity, and strength are not entirely acceptable. Qualities that are valued in men are deemed "too threatening" in women, whose attractiveness to men is based on nurturing men's creativity, not on expressing their own.

Women's feelings of inadequacy are epitomized in their feelings about their bodies. A woman can gain the approval and love of men by appearing beautiful. And yet she is also told by her mother, who communicates her own insecurities, and by the media that she is not beautiful. She must diet to rid herself of ugly fat; curl, straighten, or dye her hair; learn to apply make-up; learn how to dress; learn how to sit, stand, and walk in order to become acceptable. She must shave her legs and armpits, tweeze her eyebrows, bleach the hair on her arms and face in order to become acceptable. She must never forget perfume and deodorant. And then there is that dark space between her legs from which she bleeds each month. She must do everything she can to deny it exists. Each month she must hide the evidence of her bloody secret. She is even told to use douches or vaginal sprays to mask disgusting feminine odors. The message is clear: there is something wrong with being a woman, with her body, with being herself. Many women even learn to accept the battering of their bodies by husbands or lovers as the price they must pay to achieve acceptance. Though few women would state it so boldly, most women can understand what artist Judy Chicago meant when she wrote, "because I had a cunt, I was despised by society." [7]

For many women the experience of nothingness is a vague sense of anxiety, or an uneasy feeling that their lives have not turned out as they expected them to. Other women experience their own nothingness so deeply that they begin to doubt the value of their own lives, to consider themselves mad, or to contemplate suicide. They do not know that their experiences are shared, even common, that they are not mad, that other women feel the same way. For just as women are excluded from autonomous significance and value in men's stories, so women must even read themselves sidewise into analyses of the experience of nothingness. Women need a literature that names their pain and allows them to use the emptiness in their lives as an occasion for insight rather than as one more indication of their worthlessness. Women need stories that will tell them that their ability to face the darkness in their lives is an indication of strength, not weakness.

Women's intense perception of their own nothingness sometimes gives them acute perceptions of the larger forces of nothingness, domination, death, and destruction that operate in men's world. They may have very clear visions of the ways in which the destructive power of men operates not only in their own personal lives, but also in the larger worlds of nature and society. Even when they cannot articulate them fully, women may sense connections between their own victimization and the relentless technological devastation of the environment, the exploitation of the poor, or the bombing of villages in foreign lands. Women's identification with the victims, combined with their own feelings of powerlessness, may explain why they often fail to get involved in conventional politics, but become involved in the struggles of oppressed groups. Women's sensitivities to the currents and forces of violence may also lead them to entertain apocalyptic visions of an ultimate destruction.

The experience of nothingness often has a different quality for women than for men. Men are not conditioned to think of themselves as worthless. For them the experience of nothingness often comes after they have taken their place in the world of male power and joined the traditional hierarchies that support men's dominance in family and society. After achieving power and respect, men may come to experience their power as illusory. They may then open themselves to a deeper experience of power "not as the world knows it." As literatures of both East and West indicate, the male mystic's quest is arduous and difficult. Men have often found it difficult to give up conventional power and ego gratification to open themselves to union with the powers of being. Women, in contrast, live in a male-defined world in which culture has, for the most part, denied them access to power. The ordinary experience of women in patriarchy is akin to the experience of nothingness. Women never have what male mystics must strive to give up. Mystic insight may therefore be easier for women to achieve than men. Women may need only to strip away the ideology of patriarchy that tells them they are fulfilled as wives and mothers in order to come face to face with the nothingness they know as lack of self, lack of power, and lack of value for women in a male-centered world. To open their eyes to the emptiness of their lives requires great courage, as Mary Daly has rightly noted, but it may be easier for women since they have less to lose.

"Awakening," the title metaphor of Kate Chopin's novel, is an appropriate term for describing change in women's consciousness. "Awakening" is a metaphor that mystics and seekers frequently use to describe the experience of enlightenment—the movement from conventional notions of the meaning of life to a more direct experience of the "really real" or ground of being, from ordinary to extraordinary consciousness, from bondage to freedom. Metaphors of sleep and waking, darkness and light seem particularly appropriate for describing this sort of spiritual experience because it involves a transition in consciousness and a new perception of reality. To one who has "awakened," conventional notions of reality seem as unreal and illusory as the world of dreams does to a person abruptly aroused from sleep. To one "enlightened," it is as if she had been trying to make out clear shapes in a dark room and suddenly the lights were turned on.

"Awakening" is perhaps a more appropriate term than "conversion" for describing women's mystical experience, because "awakening" suggests that the self needs only to notice what is already there. Awakening implies that the ability to see or to know is within the self, once the sleeping draft is refused. Conversion often seems to imply that one has turned from one source of authority to another, for example, from materialism to God. It seems to be characteristic of women's awakening that the great powers, while larger than the self, are within as well as without.

Awakening also takes a distinctive form in women's experience. As we have seen, "conversion," for men, means giving up conventional, worldly, egocentric notions of power, and trusting that genuine power is rooted in union with the powers of being. For women, awakening is not so much a giving up as a gaining of power. Women often describe their awakening as a coming to self, rather than a giving up of self, as a grounding of selfhood in the powers of being, rather than a surrender of self to the powers of being.

Women's awakening to their grounding in the powers of being often occurs through a specific *mystical experience*. By mysticism in women's experience I refer to a woman's direct experience of her grounding in the powers of being that sometimes, but not always, takes the form of identification between the self and the powers of being. Besides opening them to the experience of nothingness, traditional roles may encourage in women a habitual attitude of receptivity, thus opening them to the mystical experience of union or integration with powers. In this culture women are encouraged to be receptive to the needs of others—to please or nurture parents, children, spouses, lovers. The traditional work roles of women—such as teaching and nursing—require receptivity to others. This habitual orientation toward others often encourages women to fall into what two women theologians have called a uniquely female form of sin through self-negation.[8] It is essential for women to move through self-negation and self-hatred to new affirmations of selfhood, power, and responsibility. But it is also important for women to name and cultivate the possible strengths that traditional roles have encouraged them to develop. If women's roles have made them open to certain kinds of spiritual experience, then this fact should not be denied, though neither should it be used to keep women in roles that are no longer meaningful for them.

The pattern of female development suggests one reason why mystical experiences are easier for women to achieve than men. Freudian and Jungian psychologists allege that the early infant experience of both males and females is one of identification with the mother.[9] The boundary between self and other is not recognized. As she or he begins to develop a sense of separateness, the mother-reared[10] child's first task is to define the boundaries between itself and the mother. But this process proceeds differently for boys and girls. For boys the recognition of their differences from their mothers is more total, and they organize their lives around being different from or "not like" their mothers. This encourages the development of firm—some would say rigid—ego boundaries and encourages a habit of relating to the world in which differences are accentuated. The girl, on the other hand, while recognizing her difference from her mother, still retains a sense of identification with her, for she recognizes that she is "like" her mother in being a female. This encourages her to develop less rigid ego boundaries and to think of her relationship to the world more in terms of sameness than difference. Most psychologists have tended to emphasize the positive aspects of the male model of development. In truth, both ways of developing produce different strengths and different weaknesses. If men's mode of developing gives them strong egos and a strong sense of self, it makes them less open to experiences of identification or sympathy, less likely to see other persons or beings as "like" themselves, less open to mystical experiences. And if the negative side of women's development is that they have weaker egos than men, the positive side is that identification, sympathy, and mystical experiences are easier for them to achieve.

In the literature I will be discussing, women's mystical experiences have similarities with classical descriptions of the mystical experience. William James's definition of mystical experience is useful for discussing women's mysticism, since it is based on comparisons of the mystic experience from a variety of traditions and does not have a theistic bias. He cites four characteristics of mysticism—ineffability, noetic quality, transiency, and passivity.[11] Ineffability refers to the experience's defiance of expression. Those who have had the experience always say that words can only point to it, that it can never be fully expressed in words. Sensitivity to mystic experience may be like having an ear for music. The noetic quality of the experience refers to the sense of illumination, revelation, or awakening that the experience brings. The experience is transient or brief, lasting seconds or hours, after which the person returns to normal consciousness. According to James, the fourth characteristic, passivity, describes the mystic's sense of being grasped or held by a superior power. James's notion of passivity seems to be related to the surrender of ego, which, as discussed above, may be more characteristic of men's mystical experience than women's. With reference to women's experience I would rename James's fourth characteristic union or integration. It seems to me that the mystic's experience is one of union with or integration with the power or powers of being in which neither activity nor passivity is an appropriate description. This aspect of the experience is more aptly described by the expression "life flows on within me and without me."[12] The experience is not so much one of passivity before the larger powers as it is an integration in which the self directly experiences a connection or identity between its own power and the powers of being.

R. C. Zaehner, another important theorist of mysticism, defines mysticism as an experience in which "sense perception and discursive thought are transcended in an immediate apperception of a unity lying beyond and transcending the multiplicity of the world as we know it."[13] Though stated less simply and generally, Zaehner's definition agrees in essentials with James's.

Evelyn Underhill, who has written many books on mysticism, adds to James's definition the notions that the mystical experience involves the whole self and that it leads to a transformation of the self.[14] However, her notion that the mystic's aims are always transcendental and spiritual seems to accept the split of reality into spiritual and mundane, which women's spiritual quest seeks to overcome. Moreover, her notion that the mystic's object is a living and personal object of love, a "changeless one," has a theistic ring more characteristic of Christian mysticism than the mysticism to be discussed here.

James's notion of the mystical experience as ineffable, transient, insight-producing, and leading to what I have called union or integration with the powers of being, combined with Underhill's notion that mysticism involves and transforms the whole self, is a good working definition of mysticism in women's experience. However, neither James, Zaehner, nor Underhill discusses the fact that women's grounding in the powers of being often leads to newfound *self*-awareness and *self*-confidence.

Women's mystical experiences differ from mystical experiences discussed by classical theorists in yet another important respect: the great power is often experienced in nature.[15] While James discusses examples of mysticism evoked by nature, he gives them little attention and considers them examples of "sporadic," as opposed to "cultivated," mysticism, which he values more highly. Zaehner considers nature mysticism inferior to two higher types of mysticism, the monistic and the theistic. He does, however, offer a theoretical definition of nature mysticism as involving the experience that within and without are one, a notion that fits with my conception of nature mysticism in women's experience. Since Underhill asserts as part of her central definition of mysticism that it is union with a spiritual changeless one, she too pays little attention to nature mysticism.

Simone de Beauvoir, a theorist of women's experience but not of mysticism, has noted that women often experience a transcendence in nature that is closed to them in society. "As a member of society she enters upon adult life only in becoming a woman; she pays for her liberation by an abdication. Whereas among plants and animals she is a human being; she is freed at once from her family and from the males."[16] De Beauvoir rightly calls attention to women's exclusion from culture as one reason for their mystical experiences with nature. It should also be noted that traditional cultural associations of women with nature and the conventional limitation of their sphere to children, home, and garden also encourage women to be open to mystical experiences in nature. In almost all cultures, women's bodily experiences of menstruation, pregnancy, childbirth, and lactation, combined with their cultural roles of caring for children, the sick, the dying, and the dead have led to the cultural association of women with the body and nature, and men with culture, the spirit, and transcendence.[17] Whether or not women really are closer to nature than men, cultural attitudes and cultural roles have encouraged women to develop a sense of their own affinity with nature. Poet Susan Griffin, who has explored many aspects of women's feelings of connection to nature, writes, "The earth is my sister; I love her daily grace, her silent daring . . . and I do not forget: what she is to me, what I am to her."[18]

Women's mystical experiences in nature also provide them with a sense of authentic selfhood. Feminist literary critic Annis Pratt concludes that for many women "communion with the authentic self, first achieved by the heroine in early naturistic epiphanies, becomes a touchstone by which she holds herself together in the face of destructive roles proffered to her by society."[19] Women's experiences in nature are extremely significant because they can occur in solitude when a woman feels isolated from other people and has nowhere to turn. When in the depths of despair and loneliness many women are rescued by sensing their grounding in nature.

While mystical experiences in nature frequently provide women with a sense of authentic selfhood, many also have mystical experiences in society or community. Many of the women writers I will be discussing also reflect a sensibility that I call social or communal mysticism. In this form of mysticism, the great powers to which women awaken are experienced through social groups or movements, rather than through nature. In this form of mystical insight, a specific social or political movement, such as the antiwar movement or the women's movement, is not deified or treated as the ultimate power. Instead it is recognized that great powers are revealed through such movements and that the quests for truth or justice or being which they embody are rooted in the powers of being. Social mysticism may be considered analogous to the Christian notion of "community of saints" or the Jewish "all Israel," images of a community united by its relationship to greater powers in which a mystical unity between the dead, the living, and those yet to be born is affirmed.

After a woman experiences the grounding of her quest in the powers of being, it is important for her to name her experience in words. When one woman puts her experiences into words, another woman who has kept silent, afraid of what others will think, can find validation. And when the second woman says aloud, "Yes, that was my experience too," the first woman loses some of her fear. "The dream of a common language," which Adrienne Rich has movingly depicted, is realized in the moment when two women acknowledge each other and themselves. Their act creates new possibilities of being and living for themselves and for all women. With the creation of a new language, the possibility that women will forget what they know is lessened.

Women have called the process of giving form to their experience

through words a *new naming*. Mary Daly has spoken of the Genesis
story of Adam's naming of woman and the animals as paradigmatic of
a cosmic "false naming" in which women and the world have been
named only from men's point of view.[20] As women begin to name the
world for themselves not only will they create new life possibilities for
women, they will also upset the world order that has been taken
for granted for centuries. "What would happen if one woman told
the truth about her life?" asks poet Muriel Rukeyser. "The world
would split open."[21] Women's speech has the potential to transform
the way people view the world. The subordination of women not only
has been taken for granted by philosophers and poets whose writings
have shaped Western consciousness, but the assumption of women's
secondary status also has influenced philosophers' and poets' perceptions of the nature of authority and hierarchy, and of the relation
of spirit and flesh, humanity and nature, body and soul. All of these
subtle and not-so-subtle relationships will be challenged and, I hope,
transformed as women begin to write out of their own experience.

Learning to value everything about being a woman is a key
theme in women's new naming. Women name the beauty and strength
of women's bodies and of their own particular bodies. They learn to
value the life-giving potential of their monthly bleeding and celebrate
their bodies' connections to nature. Women learn to overcome the
"false naming" and devaluing of traditional women's activities like
mothering and nurturing. They begin to name women's activities
as sources of insight, to name women's valuing of nurturance as a
power of life which women may use to transform culture, and to
celebrate those bold women who have defied conventional roles.
They begin to value solitude once avoided, and to value time alone
and "a room of one's own." They celebrate their connections with
other women and positively name them "sisterhood." Thus, far from
being trivial, the new celebration of women's bodies, powers, solitude, and connections to each other is the beginning of the end of
centuries-old patterns of self-hatred and self-negation.

Women's experiences of the power of being also have implications for their understanding of the world. Cultural attitudes toward
women cannot be changed without changing the view of the world

in which they are embedded. For example, the relationship between women's bodies and nature has been a source of cultural denigration. As women attempt to overcome this denigration, it is tempting for them to deny their connection to nature in order to assert their claim to transcendence. Indeed, Simone de Beauvoir, in her classic work *The Second Sex* asserted that women's role as birth-givers had led to their cultural entrapment in "immanence" and "species life," which de Beauvoir opposed to the truly human enterprises of "freedom" and "transcendence." In de Beauvoir's work, having a female body is seen as an impediment to the achievement of transcendence, but in a technological society, not sufficient reason to bar women from transcendence altogether. The reader of her book is left with the inescapable conclusion that being female is slightly inferior to being male.[22] If being female is not to be seen as less than being male, and if women's nature mystical experiences are to be viewed as significant, then the human connection to nature will have to be rethought.

This calls into question the traditional opposition of nature and spirit, one of the fundamental assumptions of Western thought. As Rosemary Ruether has argued, dualistic thinking—spirit or freedom versus nature, reason versus emotion (which is called irrational), soul versus body – has oppressed women.[23] Men have organized dualisms hierarchically and have associated themselves with the positive sides of the dualisms—spirit, freedom, reason, and soul—while relegating women to the negative sides of the dualisms—nature, emotion, irrationality, and the body. Moreover, philosophers have traditionally perceived these dualisms as oppositions in which the inferior continually threatens to overwhelm the superior. Hence, the name "war" is given to the relations between the spirit and the flesh, freedom and nature, man and woman, reason and emotion, and "man" is warned to remain perpetually ready to do "battle" with flesh, nature, woman, and the emotional realm. As women begin to question their historic subordination, they also challenge the adequacy of the dualistic, hierarchical, and oppositional ways of viewing the world. If women are different from but not inferior to men, then perhaps nature is different from but not inferior to spirit. Indeed, what has been called irrational— emotion, intuition, and sometimes even poetry—may not be inferior to the modes of thinking that have been called rational. And the so-called wars between the opposing sides of the dualisms may be a result of an attempt to subordinate some aspects of reality to others that is not inherent in the structure of reality itself. While other groups, including psychologists in the humanistic schools, adherents of certain Eastern meditational disciplines, and those concerned with natural health, also oppose the classical dualisms, Ruether has argued that women have a crucial role to play in their overthrow. A revaluing of the so-called negative sides of the classic dualisms and a trans-formation of the hierarchical mentality is implicit in women's quest. To put it another way, women's quest is for a wholeness in which the oppositions between body and soul, nature and spirit or freedom, rationality and emotion are overcome.

# 3. Spiritual Liberation, Social Defeat: Kate Chopin

WHEN IT WAS PUBLISHED in 1899, Kate Chopin's story of the awakening of a married woman created a scandal because of its frank treatment of sensuality and suicide.[1] Recently reclaimed as a feminist classic, *The Awakening* poses a challenge to critics because of its controversial ending. Is Edna Pontellier's suicide the triumph of a strong woman who chooses to die rather than capitulate to the constricting social mores of her time? Or is it the defeat of a woman too little aware of herself, too weak to face disappointment in her romantic fantasies and to create a life for herself alone? The distinction between spiritual and social quest is the key to resolving this question, I think. Edna's suicide reflects spiritual triumph but social defeat. And the real tragedy of the novel is that spiritual and social quests could not be united in her life. Chopin's novel shows that spiritual awakening without social support can lead to tragedy, and provides convincing testimony that women's quest must be for full spiritual and social liberation.

Edna Pontellier's awakening and search for selfhood is set against the backdrop of two contrasting and, for her, equally unacceptable, images of womanhood: the devoted, voluptuous, mother-woman, Adele Ratignolle, and the eccentric solitary artist, Mademoiselle Reisz. While she is attracted to Madame Ratignolle's Creole sensuality and the picture of domestic bliss she creates with her husband and children,

Edna recognizes that she herself is not a "mother-woman" who can find fulfillment as "ministering angel" (19).[2] Her statement to Adele that she would give her life for her children, but not her self, marks her distance from Madame Ratignolle's world. Similarly, Edna admires Mademoiselle Reisz's dedication to her piano and savors the spell she weaves with her music, but cannot accept for herself Reisz's life of solitude and bitter isolation from society. While she may not put it into these words, Edna's quest is for wholeness—for a total sexual and creative life as a woman. Like recent feminists, she implicitly rejects the choice of either a conventional sexual life in a marriage that allows no time for her to express her creativity, or the solitary spinsterhood of a woman who is devoted to her art or career. Like men, she wants both. Her refusal to accept the nineteenth-century choice offered her marks Edna's quest as a particularly modern one.

Edna's awakening is sparked by her friendship with the son of the woman who owned the cottages on Grand Isle where Edna and her family summered. Robert Lebrun, a charming young man, had not established himself in business and was known for his summer flirtations with married women. In French Creole society such attachments were not taken seriously because it was understood that the Creoles' "entire absence of prudery" was kept in check by "a lofty chastity which in the Creole woman seems to be inborn" (23). But Edna's Protestant background had not prepared her for Robert, and as Adele Ratignolle warned him, "she might make the unfortunate blunder of taking you seriously" (51). In Robert, whose feelings and even coloring were like her own, Edna imagined she had found what Adrienne Rich has called "the phantom of the man-who-would-understand, / the lost brother, the twin."[3] Women are often attracted to young men like Robert who have not fully allied themselves with the attitudes of domination and authority that characterize older men in patriarchal societies. For Edna, Robert is a welcome relief from her husband, with whom she shares no "sympathy of thought and taste" (46), "no trace of passion or excessive and fictitious warmth" (47). Unfortunately, as Edna learns later, Robert also shares with men of his type a second quality that Adrienne Rich aptly named, "a passivity we mistake / —in the desperation of our search— / for gentleness."[4]

Robert is more to Edna than the lover of romantic fantasy. He encourages her to learn to swim and thus opens her to the sea in which she discovers the infinity of her soul as well as the sensuality of her body. Their conversations prompt her to think about the meaning of her life, something married women are rarely encouraged to do. He also awakens her to the passions of her body and to the capacity for full sexual experience.

Chopin describes Edna's awakening in a passage that occurs near the beginning of the story and is repeated again at its end. The passage begins, "a certain light was beginning to dawn dimly within her,—the light which, showing the way, forbids it" (33). The dawning yet forbidding light suggests revelation, but also portends the tragedy that follows Edna's enlightenment. The passage continues:

> At that early period it served but to bewilder her. It moved her to dreams, to thoughtfulness, to the shadowy anguish which had overcome her the midnight when she had abandoned herself to tears.
> In short, Mrs. Pontellier was beginning to realize her position in the universe as a human being, and to recognize her relations as an individual to the world within and about her (33).

Here the spiritual dimension of the novel is clearly articulated: it concerns Edna's recognition of the nature and potential of her own soul and its relation to the cosmos, "the world about her." This realization seems so simple some might not call it "spiritual." But Chopin clearly intends the reader to compare Edna's awakening to those religious awakenings commonly called conversions, as is evident from her ironic comment, "this may seem like a ponderous weight of wisdom to descend upon the soul of a young woman of twenty-eight—perhaps more wisdom than the Holy Ghost is usually pleased to vouchsafe to any woman" (33–34).

The sea is the medium of Edna's awakening.[5] Walking by the sea, Edna senses the limitless potential of her soul and begins to question her life.

> But the beginning of things, of a world especially, is necessarily vague, tangled, chaotic, and exceedingly dis-

> turbing. How few of us ever emerge from such a beginning!
> How many souls perish in its tumult!
>
> The voice of the sea is seductive; never ceasing, whis-
> pering, clamoring, murmuring, inviting the soul to wander
> for a spell in abysses of solitude; to lose itself in mazes of
> inward contemplation.
>
> The voice of the sea speaks to the soul. The touch of
> the sea is sensuous, enfolding the body in its soft, close
> embrace (34).

A symbol of infinite and fearful power, the sea is also empowering. When she first learns to swim, "She did shout for joy, as with a sweeping stroke or two she lifted her body to the surface of the water. A feeling of exultation overtook her, as if some power of significant import had been given her to control the working of her body and her soul" (70). Swimming in the ocean is both a physical and spiritual experience; Edna feels control over her body *and* over her soul. Chopin alludes to the rarity of a woman's awakening when she adds, "She wanted to swim far out, where no woman had swum before" (70–71). Literally Edna is far out in the ocean, but metaphorically her social and spiritual quest carry her far beyond the social conventions that have limited women's sphere. The passage continues:

> She turned her face seaward to gather in an impression of
> space and solitude, which the vast expanse of water,
> meeting and melting with the moonlit sky, conveyed to
> her excited fancy. As she swam she seemed to be reaching
> out for the unlimited in which to lose herself (71).

Edna's experience is a classic mystical experience of temporary union with a great power, and the experience provides her with a sense of illumination.[6]

Edna's awakening reminds her of a mystical experience she had as a young girl—an experience that growing up and patriarchal religion had made her forget. She thinks of "a summer day in Kentucky, of a meadow that seemed as big as the ocean to the very little girl walking through the grass, which was higher than her waist. She threw out her arms as if swimming when she walked, beating the tall grass as one strikes out in the water" (41–42). And she recalls, "I felt as if I must walk on forever" (42). Edna's girlhood experience verifies Simone de Beauvoir's insight that adolescent girls often experience a transcendence in nature that is closed to them in society. Significantly, Edna remarks, that just after the time of the experience in the meadow, religion "took a firm hold upon me" (42), a statement revealing Chopin's ironic recognition that patriarchal religion stifles women's spirituality.

Chopin stresses that to awaken is risky. She alludes to the sea as seducing the soul to "lose itself in mazes of inward contemplation" (34), and when Edna swims out too far, she glimpses a "quick vision of death" that "smote her soul." The element of danger in Edna's experience—a portent of her suicide—is a common feature of mystic experience. Mystical experience shatters an old self, and the mystic who faces nothingness risks becoming lost there—the conventional supports of the self shattered but were lacking the revelation that could lead to the creation of a new self on the other side of nothingness. For a woman the risk is that when the patriarchal definitions of her being are stripped away, she will be faced with radical freedom; she will have no guidelines to tell her how to act. She must have courage, clear-sightedness, and awareness of the consequences of her choices or she may lose herself.

Edna's mystical experience reflects wholeness. She is not transported out of the body into a transcendent world. Instead the experience is extremely physical, even sensual, and in it she finds revealed the power of her body as well as her soul. For her physical, sexual, social, and spiritual awakening occur together.

Edna's awakening starts her on the path of women's social quest, a search for new ways of living in human community. Though not always aware of the consequences of her actions, Edna takes a series of steps, small at first, that move her far beyond the conventional woman's life she had known. Newly aware of the value of her own subjectivity, Edna begins to defy her husband openly. Leonce Pontellier is a man whose life is ordered according to the unspoken assumptions of patriarchal privilege. Though he is usually occupied with his business or his club, he considers his wife "the sole object of his existence" (11) and believes that "he loved [his children] very much" (12) when he actually pays little attention to them. He believes that he always knows what is best for his wife and often looks upon her as a "valuable piece of personal property" (4). In his world, which Edna had never directly challenged, there is no room for Edna's new awareness of the value of her own thoughts and feelings. Their first real confrontation occurs at Grand Isle on the night Edna first swims out by herself and feels her passions aroused by Mademoiselle Reisz's piano, Robert's presence, and her own strength. When her husband returns from town late, as he often did, he finds her on the front porch dozing. As usual, he asks her to come in with him, and, as usual, he expects her obedience. When she decides to stay out a bit longer, he orders her in, and she feels "her will had blazed up, stubborn and resistant" (79). This seemingly trivial incident takes on monumental proportions because it is Edna's first direct challenge to the tacit premise of their marriage—his authority.

Back in New Orleans at the end of the summer Edna continues her rebellion. She becomes negligent in her management of the servants. Instead of staying home to receive callers, she goes out for the day. Irritated at her refusal to fulfill her duties as hostess, an angry Mr. Pontellier stomps off to his club, and Edna's anger explodes in a vain attempt to crush her wedding ring. Chopin sums up the change in Edna with an understatement: "she began to do as she liked and to feel as she liked" (146). Mr. Pontellier, "a rather courteous husband so long as he met a certain tacit submissiveness in his wife" (146), is bewildered and angered by the change in his wife.

When she refuses to go on a business trip with him, Pontellier reluctantly decides to let her have her way, and sends his mother for the children, leaving Edna alone. Chopin eloquently depicts what is probably Edna's first adult experience of solitude.

> A feeling that was unfamiliar but very delicious came over her. She walked all through the house, from one room to another, as if inspecting it for the first time. She tried the various chairs and lounges, as if she had never sat and reclined upon them before . . . The flowers were like new acquaintances . . . (188).

Edna sees everything freshly. With Pontellier and his opinions out of the house, she feels free to see with her own eyes and to "experience her own experience." The simple act of deciding which chair she finds comfortable or beautiful has enormous significance—for the first time she is naming her world from her own perspective.

With Robert off in Mexico on a business venture, which is his way of avoiding his passion for her, Edna busies herself with her art. She spends most of her days drawing and receives encouragement from a local art dealer, Laidpore, who "is more and more pleased" with her work and has begun to sell it (207). Chopin says little about Edna's feelings about her work, but it is evident from her successes that Edna now views her art as more than dabbling.

During this period, Edna is preoccupied with fantasies of her reunion with Robert. Though she is developing as a person, Edna still imagines that her happiness is linked to him. But to fill her time, she makes new friends. The most important of these are Mademoiselle Reisz and Alcée Arobin. When Edna visits Mademoiselle Reisz, the lonely old eccentric pianist, she discovers that Robert is corresponding with Reisz about Edna. Besides sharing Robert's letters with her, Reisz provides Edna with a musical articulation of her new feelings and passions. On Grand Isle, Reisz's music had aroused the passions in Edna's soul, "swaying it, lashing it, as the waves daily beat upon her splendid body" (66). And in the city her music has the same effect, "her divine art seemed to reach Edna's spirit and set it free" (204).

Alcée Arobin, Edna's other new friend, is a sensual, handsome, smooth-tongued specialist in affairs with married women, who plays his role with a "manner . . . so genuine that it often deceived even himself" (201). Not imagining any sympathy of soul between them, Edna nonetheless finds Alcée attractive and succumbs to his seductions. Though she seems to have no regret about her affair with Arobin, Edna still anticipates a union of soul and body when Robert returns.

Her confidence in her own powers growing, Edna takes the decisive step of moving out of her husband's home and into a small cottage nearby. This she accomplishes with a small inheritance left by her mother and from the money she makes painting. Like Virginia Woolf after her, Chopin recognizes that women cannot gain freedom to create the world from their own experience until they are freed from emotional and financial dependence on men and from the constant interruptions of household duties and children. Edna's little house, like Woolf's "room of one's own," is a symbol for the psychic emancipation of the female mind. Edna's inheritance from her mother (not her father), like Woolf's 500 pounds a year left by a female relative, also symbolizes women's freedom from male control. Of her new home, Edna remarks, "I know I shall like it, like the feeling of freedom and independence" (208).

When Edna leaves her husband's home she plans a dinner party for a few selected friends using all the finest silver and gold, as a farewell to her life in Pontellier's house and as a symbolic expression of her control over her own destiny. At first the party is an enormous success and Edna appears imperious and triumphant, like a queen or Goddess. "There was something in her attitude, in her whole appearance when she leaned her head against the high-backed chair and spread her arms, which suggested the regal woman, the one who rules, who looks on, who stands alone" (231-232). But at the end of the party a mischievous Victor Lebrun, draped to resemble the God Eros, reminds Edna that she has not yet learned to stand alone. When he sings a lover's song that reminds her of Robert, she is angered and disheartened, and dismisses her guests.

With the move into the little house, Edna has taken enormous steps toward her social and spiritual liberation. She has freed herself psychically and financially from a domineering husband; she has begun to develop her artistic talent; she has freely expressed her sexuality. But despite these positive steps, powerful social forces are arrayed against her. There is no one who understands and supports her quest. The two other significant women characters in the book, Mademoiselle Reisz, the eccentric solitary artist, and Madame Ratignolle, the satisfied sensual "mother-woman," sympathize with aspects of Edna's quest, but neither can offer her what she needs—a sympathetic sisterhood or role model for the whole life she seeks. Madame Ratignolle constantly reminds Edna of her duties as a mother and wife. And shortly after returning to New Orleans, Edna realizes that she can never be like her friend whose "domestic harmony" appears to Edna as a "colorless existence which never uplifted its possessor beyond the region of blind contentment, in which no moment of anguish ever visited her soul, in which she would have the taste of life's delirium" (145). Mademoiselle Reisz, though she sympathizes with Edna's artistic impulses and desire to escape her confining marriage, and even understands her love for Robert, warns Edna to expect a life of isolation if she chooses to flout convention. Her words to Edna— "The bird that would soar above the level plain of tradition and prejudice must have strong wings. It is a sad spectacle to see the weaklings bruised, exhausted, fluttering back to earth" (217)—are a foreshadowing of Edna's tragic end. Reisz's fear is realistic, but she equates women's quest with social isolation, and offers no words that might aid Edna in her quest for a full and free sexual and artistic life.

The male characters in the novel also hold conventional values that prevent them from understanding Edna's quest. Edna's husband at first opposes her newly expressed willfulness and then adopts an attitude of benign tolerance, expecting that she will get over her discontent. Alcée, her lover, though tender and thoughtful, is a conventional ladies' man. Even Robert, whom Edna fancies sympathizes with her awakening, is weak and conventional.

A third force opposing Edna's quest is her own insufficient self-consciousness and dedication in both her art and her life. Though her devotion to her art deepens, Mademoiselle Reisz rightly senses that Edna is not sufficiently dedicated to it to make it her whole life. Edna also lacks self-conscious awareness of the risks she is taking in her life and the consequences she may have to face. Chopin frequently describes Edna *after* her awakening as acting on impulse or drifting through her days as if in a dream. She seems to lack a sense of perspective on her life. One day she is despondent, the next wildly hopeful. Mademoiselle Reisz remarks directly on this quality in Edna when she says, "You seem to act without a certain amount of reflection which is necessary in this life" (250).

Finally there is the unresolved question of the children. They are away with grandparents for the summer, but eventually they must return—their presence challenging Edna's independence and unconventional behavior. In the closed Southern Catholic society of New Orleans in 1899, divorce was not tolerated and knowledge of Edna's scandalous sexual behavior would have made her children social outcasts. Though Edna had said she would not sacrifice herself for her children, she had not considered whether she would be willing to sacrifice their future happiness for her own.

The opposing forces of liberation and defeat in Edna's life are brought to a quick resolution when Robert returns to New Orleans. Though he apparently has returned because of Edna, he is still indecisive. After having been in town for several days without contacting her, he unexpectedly meets her at Mademoiselle Reisz's. When their evening together is interrupted by the appearance of Arobin, he leaves. A few days later they again meet by chance at a small restaurant. Returning with Edna to her little house, he declares his love and his desire to marry her if Pontellier would set her free. Edna's protestation, "I am no longer one of Mr. Pontellier's possessions to dispose of or not. I give myself where I choose" (282), a strong statement of her independence, only shocks him. At that point, the maid interrupts to tell Edna that Madame Ratignolle is about to give birth, and Edna remembers her promise to go to her. When she returns, Robert has fled, leaving a note that says only, "Good-by—because I love you" (294).

The vision of Adele giving birth is a "scene torture," which inspires in Edna "an inward agony, with a flaming, outspoken revolt against the ways of Nature" (288). After giving birth, Adele reminds Edna of her own bondage to nature. "Think of the children, Edna" (289), she whispers. The next day Edna, thinking of her children and her recent abandonment by Robert, returns to Grand Isle, swims out into the sea, and drowns.

The conclusion of *The Awakening* in Edna's death in the sea has provoked contradictory responses from critics. Some have seen it as a triumphal act; others, as a defeat. Still others view Chopin's treatment of Edna's suicide as purposefully ambiguous.[7]

Chopin surrounds Edna's death with contradictory symbols of defeat and rebirth. This makes it difficult to assess the meaning of Edna's final act and accounts for the various readings proposed. There is also the further complication that it is not clear whether Edna's death is consciously chosen suicide or whether it, like much else in Edna's life, is simply drifted into.

Edna's purpose in going to Grand Isle the day she dies is not clear. The day before, she had just witnessed the torture scene of the birth of Madame Ratignolle's child and been reminded to "think of the children." This shocks Edna into a recognition that she cannot avoid the issue of her children indefinitely. When she returns to her little house to discover that Robert has left, she feels "faint" and stays awake all night. When next we see Edna, she is at Grand Isle, the scene of her awakening, telling Victor she has come "for no purpose but to rest" (297). This statement and her request for some fish for her dinner indicate that she probably had not planned suicide when she came to the island. Later, however, Chopin suggests the suicide was contemplated when she says that the night before the children appeared before Edna like antagonists, but "she knew a way to elude them" (300). Still, when Edna goes down to the beach Chopin tells us "she was not thinking of these things" (300). It seems reasonable to conclude that the thought of suicide had crossed Edna's mind the night before, but that she had no firmly conceived plan to take her life when she returned to Grand Isle. Edna was also motivated to return to Grand Isle, the site of her freedom, to reaffirm her commitment to her spiritual and social quests, and apparently followed her impulse to go to the sea without sorting out her purpose.

The last chapter of the book is filled with dual imagery of defeat and rebirth. The key symbol of defeat is the image of the "bird with the broken wing," which Edna sees "reeling, fluttering, circling disabled down, down to the water" (301) as she makes her way to the beach. This image recalls Mademoiselle Reisz's earlier statement to Edna that the bird who would soar above convention must have strong wings and confirms Reisz's fear that Edna's wings are not strong enough to survive the struggles she must face. Moreover, just before the image of the bird with the broken wing appears, the passage about the voice of the sea "seductive, never ceasing, whispering, clamoring, murmuring" is repeated, but it concludes simply with a repetition of the warning that the sea invites the soul to "wander in abysses of solitude" (300). The earlier qualification "for a spell" is omitted, and the reader senses that Edna has perhaps lost her soul permanently in the abyss of solitude—the risk that Chopin had hinted at earlier. But this imagery of defeat is followed by extremely positive imagery of rebirth. Edna casts off her clothing and "for the first time in her life she stood naked in the open air, at the mercy of the sun . . . She felt like some new-born creature, opening its eyes in a familiar world that it had never known" (301). Such a passage would not appear in a work whose author intended the reader to see her character as defeated.

In the concluding paragraphs of the novel conflicting imagery abounds. Edna enters the sea and swims far out. She remembers her earlier terror of death, but does not look back. She recalls the blue grass meadow, image of her childhood experience of mystical liberation, and affirms that her husband and children will never possess her body and soul. This imagery seems to confirm the interpretation of her death as a positive act, an affirmation of the spiritual liberation she has known. But then negative images reappear as Edna remembers how Mademoiselle Reisz will sneer at her because she does not have the courage to dare and defy. And her final thoughts are equally conflicting. She thinks first of father and sister—images of censure, of a dog chained to a tree—an image of bondage, of the cavalry officer she once had a crush on—a romantic delusion, but finally of the hum of bees and the musky odor of pinks—images of natural fertility, harmony, and completion.

What is the meaning of the conflicting imagery at the end of the novel? Is Edna a weak-willed woman in the grip of romantic delusions, defeated by her own lack of self-consciousness, as some critics have alleged? Or is she, on the other hand, a feminist heroine who defies convention to return to the scene of her awakening and liberation, and valiantly chooses death rather than a return to a conventional life that would mean psychic and spiritual death?

The interpretation of defeat denies the central event of the novel—Edna's awakening in the sea and the sea's positive meaning for her—and also fails to make sense of the rebirth imagery at the end of the novel. But the interpretation of triumph also ignores an important element of the novel—Edna's lack of full self-consciousness and her weakness, symbolized in the image of the bird with the broken wing. How can the reader resolve this dilemma and provide a satisfactory interpretation of the conclusion of the novel?

I suggest that the clue lies in the distinction between spiritual and social quest. Edna's suicide is a spiritual triumph but a social defeat. In it she states, even if only partially consciously, that no one will possess her body and soul, and affirms her awakening by returning to the sea where it occurred. As Per Seyersted, Chopin's biographer, says, "when the apparently defeated Edna takes off her clothes . . . it symbolizes a victory of self-knowledge and authenticity as she fully becomes herself." And as he also notes, "nothing can hinder Edna from being intimately joined with the universe."[8] But Edna's suicide is also social defeat in that by choosing death she admits that she cannot find a way to translate her spiritual awareness of her freedom and infinite possibilities into life and relationships with others. From this stand-point the real tragedy of the novel is that the spiritual and social quests cannot be realized together. This ambiguous and tragic ending seems to reflect Chopin's view that the path to women's liberation is far more difficult and complex than some nineteenth-century feminists had alleged and requires a soul stronger than many women possess.[9]

This interpretation also provides a way of judging Chopin's achievement in *The Awakening* from the perspective of women's need for new stories. The strength of the novel is Chopin's convincing portrayal of a woman's awakening, including her awareness of the spiritual dimensions of that awakening and her unflinching recognition of the powers arrayed against the awakening of women in her society. In my view, Chopin's choice of physical death for her character rather than the alternative of spiritual death by returning to a conventional life reflects Chopin's courageous affirmation of women's awakening. But the weakness of the novel is that Chopin could not envision any person who could give Edna support in her quest nor imagine any alternative for Edna other than spiritual or physical death.

The ending of *The Awakening* may have been realistic for its times, but readers who recognize the importance of stories in shaping lives have a right to ask more of a novelist than realism.[10] This is not to say that all books must have happy endings. But it is to acknowledge that, like Doris Lessing's Martha Quest, women ask literature to provide images of a woman who is "a person" they seek to become. These images may be difficult to imagine, yet life is not entirely lacking in examples of women who are persons. One task facing women writers is to write stories in which the spiritual and social quest can be combined in the life of a living, realistic woman. And also, one task facing readers is not to be fully satisfied with women's literature until it does so.

# 4. Refusing to Be Victim: Margaret Atwood

THE SPIRITUAL QUEST of the unnamed protagonist of *Surfacing* begins with her return to the Canadian wilderness, where she had lived as a child. Ostensibly, the protagonist is in search of her missing father, who is presumed dead. But the search is really for her missing parents, her mother having died a few years earlier, and for the power she feels it was their duty to have communicated to her. The external detective story of the protagonist's search for her father is paralleled by an internal search—half obscured by her obsession with her father—to discover how she lost the ability to feel. The scene of the mystery is strewn with false clues from her fictitious memories, which she created to shield herself from the pain of confronting her true past. While the protagonist's interest remains focused on her father's disappearance, the reader struggles to make sense of the inconsistencies in her story about her marriage, husband, and child. Why couldn't she return home after the wedding? Why did she hide the child from her parents? Why is she obsessed with the bizarre image of her brother floating just below the surface of the water, a near drowning that occurred before she was born? The unraveling of her father's mystery awakens her to the powers that enlighten her, but the unraveling of her own mystery is the key to the redemption she seeks. The two mysteries intersect when she recognizes that "it was no longer his death but my own that concerned me" (123).[1]

Even at the beginning of the journey the protagonist recognizes that she has experienced a death. Like the three friends, Anna, David,

41

and Joe, who accompany her, she is completely cut off from her past: "Any one of us could have amnesia for years and the others wouldn't notice" (33). She has also lost the ability to experience normal feelings. She recalls that her current man-friend, Joe, was impressed by her coolness the first time they made love. She, on the other hand, found her behavior unremarkable because she did not feel anything. She is tortured by Joe's demand that she say she love him because she does not believe the word has any meaning.

The protagonist's alienation from her feelings is reflected in her dispassionate voice. Everything is seen; nothing is felt. The small town, the cabin in the woods where she grew up, her three friends, even her memories are accurately recorded—or so it seems. Occasionally she slips, as when she says, "I keep my outside hand on the [car] door . . . so I can get out quickly if I have to" (8), causing the reader to ask whether she is similarly defensive about her life, perhaps censoring her story. The reader is suspicious when the protagonist reports how she copes with the pain of seeing the town of her childhood changed: "I bite down into the cone and I can't feel anything for a minute but the knife-hard pain up the side of my face. Anesthesia, that's one technique: if it hurts invent a different pain" (13). How much unacknowledged anesthesia, the reader wonders, does the protagonist use? Might her whole story be a shield from a pain she wishes to deny?

The protagonist's inability to feel is paralleled by an inability to act. Her selective vision holds fast to the illusion that she is helpless and "they" do things to her. Hurt and angry that her parents died before endowing her with their power, she accuses them of having hurt her. "They have no right to get old" (9), she complains, remaining blind to the pain her abrupt departure from home doubtless caused them. Always conscious of how she might be hurt, she remains oblivious to her power to hurt others. Moreover, as the reader later discovers, she studiously avoids confronting the center of her pain, the place where she lost the ability to feel and to act—her betrayal by the first man she loved.

Unable to come to terms with his violation of her self and her body she obsessively focuses her attention on the violation of the Canadian wilderness by the men she calls "Americans," some of whom turn out to be Canadians. In *Surfacing,* the image of Canada victimized by Americans is a mirror of the protagonist's victimization by men.[2] The conflict between Americans in powerboats and Canadians in canoes[3]—one apparently stronger but alienated from nature, the other seemingly weaker but in tune with it—becomes a cover for her own pain. She identifies with Canada, the wilderness, innocent, virgin, and violated by nameless American men. Her illusion that the wilderness has no power to recover from American violation prevents her from realizing her own power to overcome her sense of violation. Though the wilderness initially deflects her vision, in the end it will provide the key, the revelation that releases her power.

Though the protagonist continually imagines herself as powerless, she is extraordinarily concerned with power. Anything out of the ordinary—Madame with one hand, a purple bean at the top of a high pole, the cool blue lake, a white mushroom, the toes of saints—all are seen as harboring magical power. To her, religion and magic are one—a view modern Westerners have often associated with children or people they call primitives. Eventually the protagonist's sense of the magic-religious powers resident in things will become a key to revelations that enable her to contact the source of her power.

At first, however, the protagonist seeks her lost power in the wrong places. Realizing that she lost the ability to feel somewhere in the past, she imagines that a simple return to childhood will provide the answer. Searching through old scrapbooks kept by her mother, she discovers that she looked normal in all the pictures—no clues there. There is a clue in the drawings from her childhood—hers of eggs and bunnies, everything peaceful, her brother's of airplanes and bombs—but she cannot quite fathom it. Another clue surfaces from the garden. She remembers that once she thought a certain purple bean on a high pole was a source of power. She says she is glad the bean did not give power to her because "if I'd turned out like the others with power I would have been evil" (41). Her association of power with evil and her dissociation of herself from both reflect a typical female delusion of innocence. Hiding from her complicity in evil feeds a false belief that she can do nothing but witness her victimization. In order to regain her power the protagonist must realize that she does not live in a world where only others have power or do evil. An unexpected thing, the sight of a dead heron strung up on a tree, monument to some "American" victory, mediates revelation.

The reaction of the protagonist and her friends to the dead heron, symbol of purposeless killing, reveals some truth about each of them. Anna's weakness is evident when she holds her nose, not from any real feeling, but simply to make an impression on the men. David's concern to preserve the Canadian wilderness from crass commercialism is revealed as mere rhetoric when he and Joe film the bird, trapping its humiliation while distancing themselves with their "art." Only the protagonist realizes the enormity of the crime as she imagines the heron in its natural habitat killing its appointed food with effortless grace. She identifies herself with the bird, wondering "what part of them the heron was, that they need so much to kill it" (137), but she does nothing to protect the heron from further humiliation.

When they pass the spot again, a day later, the sight of the heron mediates the knowledge the protagonist requires to escape her passive sense of victimization, the delusion of her childhood innocence. For her the heron is sacred object, mediator, like Christ to the Christian. Seeing it again, she realizes that her passivity is not innocence. She does not live in a world of eggs and bunnies; she did not escape the evil others are immersed in. "I felt a sickening complicity, sticky as glue, blood on my hands, as though I had been there and watched without saying No or doing anything to stop it" (150). Memories of her active participation in acts of cruelty equally senseless surface in her as she remembers how she and her brother used to throw the "bad kind" of leeches into the fire. She realizes there is no innocence in childhood. "To become like a little child again, a barbarian, a vandal: it was in us too, it was innate. A thing closed in my head, hand, synapse, cutting off my escape" (152). Though she feels trapped, recognizing her guilt and responsibility is a step toward claiming her power to refuse to be a victim.

With the path to redemption through childhood closed, the protagonist decides the clue to her redemption lies in deciphering her father's final obsession—a series of unintelligible drawings and marks on maps. At first she fears he had gone mad and wandered off into the woods, but then she discovers he was copying Indian paintings and marking their locations on maps. She goes in search of the paintings to verify his sanity and her own. Deciding that the painting she seeks is submerged underwater, she dives deep into the lake to look for it. Instead of a painting, she discovers an image from her past: "It was there but it wasn't a painting, it wasn't on the rock. It was below me, drifting towards me from the furthest level where there was no life, a dark oval trailing limbs. It was blurred but it had eyes, they were open, it was something I knew about, a dead thing, it was dead" (162). Seeing the body of her father[4] forces her to acknowledge he is dead. The mystery of her father's death solved, his image becomes a clue to her own mystery, her own death. The open eyes of his corpse remind her of the bizarre image of her brother's near drowning, but with a shock she recognizes, "it wasn't ever my brother I'd been remembering" (163). The thing approaching becomes the image of her aborted fetus "drowned in air" (163). This revelation unlocks the mystery of the confusing stories of husband, child, marriage. The childbirth was an abortion; the wedding day—the day of the abortion; the husband—the lover who told her to have the abortion. "It wasn't a wedding, there were no pigeons, the post office and the lawn were in another part of the city" (164), she remembers, finally accepting the truth about her first love affair.

The protagonist sees the fetus as a living thing, not yet a child, but an animal deserving protection like the heron. Wanting to convince her to have the abortion, her lover "said it wasn't a person, only an animal." Now she realizes, "I should have seen that it was no different, it was hiding in me as if in a burrow and instead of granting it sanctuary I let them catch it" (165). She views her abortion as no more or less a crime than the murder of the heron, but her guilt is more direct, because the creature was in her body. As the knowledge of her complicity in a killing comes to her, she realizes why she hid her past in false memories. "It was all real enough, it was enough reality forever, I couldn't accept it, that mutilation, ruin I'd made, I needed a different version" (164). She understands, too, that the anesthesia of false memory is no escape, but rather the beginning of a fatal disease: blocked feelings do not go away; they fester inside. "Since then I'd carried that death around inside me, layering it over, a cyst, a tumor, black pearl" (165). Her ability to accept the painful truth about the past counteracts the anesthesia, abolishes the need for false stories to cover up true pain. By allowing herself to feel pain, she unblocks her feelings and contacts her energy and power. "Feeling was beginning to seep back into me, I tingled like a foot that's been asleep" (166-167).

The protagonist sees this new self-knowledge for what it is—a revelation from great powers. "These gods, here on the shore or in the water, unacknowledged or forgotten, were the only ones who had ever given me anything I needed . . . The Indians did not own salvation but they had once known where it lived" (165-166). In the presence of great powers, she feels the need to worship. She leaves her sweatshirt as a thank offering to the gods whose names she does not know but whose power she has felt.

She correctly understands that her redemption comes from facing the truth and accepting the pain, guilt, and responsibility it entails. With this act, the protagonist also divorces herself from the interpretations men use to justify their crimes. She no longer believes killing can be justified as "sport." She rejects her brother's distinction between "good" leeches that deserve to live and "bad" leeches that deserve to die. She rejects her lover's distinction between "good" (legitimate) fetuses that grow up to have birthday parties and "bad" (illegitimate) fetuses that must be killed. The protagonist is allowing her own feeling, not male "morality," to define reality for her.

The revelations that come to the protagonist through the heron and the underwater image of death provide her with the knowledge that unlocks her past, but she finds the revelation incomplete. Her father's "were the gods of the head, antlers rooted in the brain" (174). She believes a gift from her mother must complement her father's gift—"Not only how to see but how to act" (174). Searching again for something out of the ordinary to provide guidance, she senses power in one of the scrapbooks her mother had made. Heavy and warm, the scrapbook opens to a picture the protagonist had drawn as a child of "a woman with a round moon stomach: the baby was sitting up inside her gazing out" (180-181). Her mother's gift is a reminder of the powers of her body. Though the gifts of the parents reflect a traditional stereotyping of men with the mind, women with the body, the protagonist incorporates both gifts and transcends the limitations of her parents' lives.

That night she conceives a child by Joe with the moon, a Goddess symbol, on her left. In a heightened state of awareness she feels "my lost child surfacing within me, forgiving me, rising from the lake where it has been prisoned for so long . . . it buds, it sends out fronds" (187). As she conceives, the protagonist resembles the Virgin Mother Goddesses of old: at one with nature and her sexual power, in tune with the rhythms of the moon, complete in herself, the male being incidental.[5]

The protagonist's extraordinary insight and sense of her power alienates her from her friends. She realizes that if she wishes to pursue the revelations and experience the powers more deeply, she must choose the isolation of the visionary quest. She can't stay with people because "they'd had their chance but they had turned against the gods, and it was time for me to choose sides" (176). When the time to leave the island comes, she hides, escaping from her friends. "I am by myself; this is what I wanted, to stay here alone" (196). "The truth is here" (197). The choice of solitude is not so much a rejection of community as a recognition that certain experiences and truths are so alien to ordinary consciousness that the individual must withdraw in order to experience them.

After the others have left, the protagonist has time and space to plumb more deeply the knowledge and experience that has been given her. Lying alone at the bottom of her canoe she has a vision of the great powers of the universe, the gods who have guided her journey: "Through the trees the sun glances; the swamp around me smolders, energy of decay turning to growth, green fire. I remember the heron; by now it will be insects, frogs, fish, other herons" (194). The great powers of the universe transform the swamp; they transform the heron from death to life. The life power rises from death. This is the meaning of the incredible words she had spoken earlier, "nothing has died, everything is alive, everything is waiting to become alive" (182).

The protagonist recognizes her body as both *revelation* and *incarnation* of the great powers of life and death. "My body also changes, the creature in me, plant-animal, sends out filaments in me; I ferry it secure between death and life, I multiply" (194). The female experience of the transformation of parts of her body into plant, animal, and infant is perhaps the most complete human incarnation of the great powers. The protagonist's vision of the universal transformative energy of life into death and death into life is reflected in her characteristic perception of the fluidity of the boundaries between objects, plants, animals, humans. Joe has "fur" like a bear, canoers are "amphibian," the fetus is "plant-animal" sending out "filaments."

After her vision, the protagonist enters the final phase of her visionary journey: transformation itself. She realizes that she can see her dead parents, and perhaps the gods themselves, if she follows the path she is beginning to sense. "The gods, their likenesses: to see them in their true shape is fatal. While you are human; but after the transformation they could be reached" (181). Her transformation is frightening. Though she knows it is beyond "any rational point of view" (196), it is neither mad nor illogical. Whereas before she had abandoned false memories, now she will give up all identity as a human. Before she had experienced the fetus transforming her body, now she will change herself into a different state.

She ritually breaks her connections to the human world—burning or purifying clothing, books, one of everything in the cabin. She is purified and transformed by immersion in the lake. Like the fetus in her womb, she changes in water. "The earth rotates, holding my body down as it holds the moon; the sun pounds in the sky, red flames pulsing from it, searing away the wrong form that encases me" (206). The powers guide her away from the garden, the house, into the woods. She becomes wild. She is animal: "I hollow a lair near the woodpile, dry leaves underneath and dead branches leaned over" (207). Having undergone transformation, she experiences mystical identification with all forms of life: "Leopard frog with green spots and gold-rimmed eyes, ancestor. It includes me, it shines, nothing moves but its throat breathing" (208). She experiences direct union with the great powers of life and death in nature. All boundaries between herself and other forms of life are abolished. She *becomes the transformative energy:* "I lean against a tree, I am a tree leaning . . . I am not an animal or a tree, I am the thing in which the trees and animals move and grow" (210).

Later she sees a vision of her mother feeding the birds; then her mother disappears, the birds remain. She is translated. This vision confirms her sense that her mother's gift is connection to nature. As Barbara Hill Rigney says, "Almost witchlike, with her long hair and wearing her magically powerful leather jacket, the mother feeds wild birds from her hand, charms a bear, and is in tune with the seasons."[6] In a similar vein, Adrienne Rich calls the mother as she appears "Mistress of the Animals."[7]

The next day she sees what her father saw. What he has seen "gazes at me with its yellow eyes, wolf's eyes, depthless but lambent as the eyes of animals seen at night in the car headlights" (216). The eyes of the wolf remind her that her father's gift is the power of seeing, or insight. The protagonist is terrified as she realizes that in the state of transformation individual human identity has no meaning. Her father's vision is impersonal, but it is also strangely comforting because it means that the life power survives a particular identity. With the vision of the parents, the protagonist's circle is complete. Her parents' power has been communicated to her.

The vision granted, the gods then retreat into "the earth, the air, the water, wherever they were when I summoned them" (218). Translated back to human form, the protagonist returns to the cabin and opens a can of beans, symbolizing her return to modern human life. Though she is no longer in direct contact with the powers, she has gained wisdom and consciousness of her own power through her encounter with them. She marks her new power with a declaration: "This above all, to refuse to be a victim . . . give up the old belief that I am powerless" (222). The source of her newly discovered power is twofold. First, she renounces the fictitious memories that held together her delusions of innocence and powerlessness. Letting go and allowing her true past to surface is itself a source of tremendous energy. Second, her grounding in her own past and in the powers of the universe provides her with a sense of authentic selfhood.

Though Atwood has effectively portrayed a woman's spiritual quest, she has left the question of its integration with the social quest open. It seems likely that the protagonist, now pregnant, will return to the city with Joe and attempt to reconstruct their relationship on the basis of her recovered ability to feel. The potential for a deeper relationship with Joe is "a possibility which wasn't there at the outset."[8] But it remains an unexplored possibility. Will Joe understand how she has changed? Will he assume equal responsibility for the care of their child? Will he view her work and personal growth as being as important as his own? Atwood's failure to address such questions makes Marge Piercy skeptical that the protagonist has achieved power at all. Using a social or political definition of power, she objects, "Power exists and some have it."[9] To Piercy, Atwood's protagonist might reply, "Power exists in many more forms than are usually recognized. I have gained power by experiencing my grounding in the great transformative powers of the universe. I don't know yet how I will translate my power into social and political forms. But you cannot deny that I have gained power." Atwood's protagonist has experienced a spiritual and psychological transformation that will give her the inner strength to change her social and political relationships. She no longer sees herself as inevitably powerless and victimized. And since Atwood's story is set in the 1970s, not the 1890s, the reader has some reason to hope that her quest to integrate the spiritual and the social will be more successful than Edna Pontellier's. I am not as uneasy about Atwood's protagonist's future as Piercy. But like her, I recognize the need for stories that describe how the woman who has awakened will live in the social world. Still, I wish Piercy had understood more clearly the contribution novels like *Surfacing* make to women's total quest: by naming anew the great powers and women's grounding in them, such novels provide women with alternatives to patriarchal notions of power that can aid their struggle to change the social world.

The newly named power, the transformative energy of life to death and death to life in *Surfacing*, is, of course, not new to the historian of religions. Atwood believes that her protagonist has discovered the great power worshiped by the Canadian Indians. Many tribal and ancient peoples, both men and women, have worshiped similar powers.[10] However, as Ruether has shown, when societies become urbanized, the culture-creating males celebrate their relative freedom from the body and nature in myth, symbol, philosophy, and theology. The traditional values derived from the body and nature then become identified primarily with women, both because women's close relation to the body and nature is evident in their traditional roles of child-bearing and nurture of the young and because the culture-creating males identify the traditional values their culture has transcended with the other, woman.[11] This development produces the paradox that the surfacing of female values in alienated urban cultures may also be a return to *some*—but not all—of the values of traditional tribal or less urbanized cultures. Even the experience of connection to nature as a life and death power may reflect a particularly female viewpoint in modern culture. Western male heroes commonly envision nature as something that must be conquered or as inert matter that can be shaped to their purposes. A woman's experience of the intertwining of life and death processes in pregnancy and childbirth—the fetus might die or its movement toward life might kill her—seems to encourage in her a realistic acceptance of death as an element in all life processes.

Tribal and ancient peoples who worshiped natural powers such as those represented in *Surfacing* knew that the close connection of life and death in the hunting and agricultural cycles and in the birth processes was a reflection of the interpenetration of life and death in all natural processes. They knew the hunted or domesticated animal and the wild plant or crop as sacred sacrifices to human life. But in Christianity, the transformative mysteries of birth and the earth were spiritualized and the notion of sacrifice was limited to Christ's death for the sins of humankind. Atwood's protagonist reverses this spiritualization when she intuits, "the animals die that we may live . . . we are the eaters of death, dead Christ-flesh resurrecting inside us . . . Canned spam, canned Jesus . . . but we refuse to worship" (160). Though speaking irreverently, the protagonist is expressing her sense that the ultimate mystery of life and death is reflected in the process of eating. Indeed the original guilt may be that we must kill to live. By showing how the ancient sense of the mysteries of life and death emerges in the consciousness of a thoroughly modern woman, Atwood has done more than nostalgically recall an ancient world view. She has suggested a direction for the transformation of modern consciousness that would be beneficial for women and all life. Reverence for the human connection to natural processes would create an atmosphere in which the natural functions of women's bodies would be celebrated rather than ignored or treated as sources of shame. Menstruation, childbirth, and menopause might once again be viewed as religiously significant events.[12] And while it would not provide solutions to all the complex problems that arise in modern technological societies, a new naming of humankind's grounding in nature might create an atmosphere, or in Crites's terms, an "orientation," in which solutions to the ecological crisis could be developed.

The issue of abortion raised by the novel provides a crucial test of the viability of the novel's vision for women's quest. The affirmation of a woman's right to control her own body and to choose abortion has been fundamental in the women's movement. And the question naturally arises: Does Atwood's protagonist's vision of her connection to nature mean that women must not have abortions but must give birth over and over again, "naturally"? A careful reading of the novel's vision suggests that this would be the wrong conclusion to draw. The novel compares the fetus in the womb to an animal in a burrow and suggests the comparison of the termination of a pregnancy to the killing of an animal living in one's body. The novel suggests that no killing should be undertaken lightly, but it also recognizes that some must die so that others may live. The protagonist's abortion was wrong for her because she did not choose it herself, but allowed her lover to choose it for his own personal convenience and because she did not allow herself to feel the sense of loss that will naturally be felt when a life is taken. The novel does not suggest that abortion is wrong, but it does suggest that abortion is not a matter of little consequence. The woman who decides that she must have an abortion should recognize, as she does in eating, that some deaths are necessary for other life and that the proper response to the sacrifice of one life for another is worship and gratitude.

The emergence of a powerful vision of women's connection to nature in a novel of women's spiritual quest seems to suggest that women can achieve power through the acceptance of female biological roles. The traditional identification of women and nature that has been a legacy of oppression can also be a potential source of power and vision. As one critic has written, to entirely reject the identification of women with the body and nature might be "to neglect that part of ourselves we have been left to cultivate and to buy into that very polarization [of culture and nature] of which we have been the primary victims."[13] More importantly, it may lead to the kind of psychic suicide that the first part of *Surfacing* portrays.

It seems to me that women must positively name the power that resides in their bodies and their sense of closeness to nature and use this new naming to transform the pervasive cultural and religious devaluation of nature and the body. Atwood's novel suggests that the opposition of spirit and body, nature and person, which is endemic in Western culture, is neither necessary nor salutary; that spiritual insight surfaces through attention to the body; and that the achievement of authentic selfhood and power depends on understanding one's grounding in nature and natural energies.

# 5. From Motherhood to Prophecy: Doris Lessing

DORIS LESSING'S immense and unwieldy five-volume series, *The Children of Violence,* charts a spiritual journey from a woman's perspective.[1] Though Lessing's intention was to write about a generation, in choosing Martha Quest as the heroine of her story she made women's experience central in it.[2] Martha's quest begins in an experience of nothingness. It is uniquely shaped by her experience of motherhood, and her guide on her journey is another woman, Lynda, through whom Martha incorporates the dark side of women's experience. Because Martha's story draws connections between women's ordinary experience and spiritual vision, it can aid other women in their quests. Indeed *The Four-Gated City,* the last volume in the Martha Quest series, might be compared to a Sufi "teaching story," which, as Lessing has written, is designed to assist "the interior movement of the human mind."[3]

At the beginning of *Martha Quest,* the first novel in the series, Martha recognizes that she lacks a role model for a positive self-image. She says to herself:

> She would *not* be like Mrs. Van Rensberg, a fat and earthy housekeeping woman; she would *not* be bitter and nagging and dissatisfied, like her mother. But then, who was she to be like? Her mind turned to the heroines she had been offered, and discarded them. (*MQ,* 10)

55

Through Martha, Lessing accurately states the problem of women in the modern world: they do not have images and models of self with which to shape their identities, chart their experiences. Vaguely aware that the old patterns will not work for her, Martha nonetheless drifts through a conventional marriage and a half-planned pregnancy. As she thinks of leaving her husband and children, Martha again searches for an image if not "in literature, which evaded these problems, then in life, that woman . . . Martha described vaguely but to her own satisfaction as 'a person'" (*PM*, 206). Inability to find an image of self makes women especially vulnerable to that experience of nothingness described by Michael Novak as "the emptiness, formlessness, and chaos at the center of human consciousness."[4]

Though Martha suffers from not having an image of self, she has a capacity within her that enables her to survive the experience of nothingness. A "detached observer, felt perhaps as a clear-lit space situated just behind the forehead" (*MQ*, 8), which Martha calls the "watcher," provides her with objectivity on herself, allows her to step back, to assess.

One of the ironic features of Martha's quest is that from the beginning she has capacities to gain transcendence, but she fails to use them to shape her life because she does not "remember" them. Lessing is fascinated by the process of knowing. What interests her is that a person can know something and yet not know it in a meaningful way. The long detours in Martha's process of self-knowledge reflect this mysterious alternation of forgetting and remembering. Not remembering transcendent experiences is a common human problem, but it is intensified for women who have no stories, models, or guides to remind them of what they know.

From the earliest stage of her journey, Martha is in touch with experiences of transcendence, but she fails to recognize them. One of these experiences is Martha's mystical integration with the veld as she walks home alone from town (*MQ*, 50-53). The experience begins as Martha becomes conscious of complete freedom while walking in the veld and at the same time aware that she is losing the feeling of freedom. Joy and sadness produce a fleeting sensation of melancholy. Then Martha's attention shifts to the beauty of the trees in the evening

light. She comes upon a rise and sees the sight in a new way, which
"caused her to forget everything else" (*MQ*, 51). As she carefully takes
in each aspect of the view, she feels herself moving to a new level of
experience. The experience includes three stages. First Martha feels
a sense of integration with the animals, the grasses, nature around
her. Then the flow of unity stops for a moment, and in that moment
Martha recognizes her "smallness, the unimportance of humanity"
(*MQ*, 52-53). Third, she feels called to accept a new understanding of
her place in the universe. The description of Martha's movement between levels of consciousness is one of the finest aspects of Lessing's
work.

> Suddenly the feeling in Martha deepened, and as it did so
> she knew she had forgotten, as always, that what she had
> been waiting for like a revelation was a pain, not a happi-
> ness; what she remembered, always, was the exaltation and
> the achievement, what she forgot was this difficult birth
> into  tate of mind . . .
> There was certainly a definite point at which the thing
> began. It was not; then it was suddenly inescapable, and
> nothing could have frightened it away (*MQ*, 52).
> . . .
> Already the thing was sliding backwards, becoming a whole
> in her mind, instead of a process; the memory was changing,
> so that it was with nostalgia that she longed "to try again"
> (*MQ*, 53).

The experience comes over Martha in a flash. It is not there, then it is
there, then it slips away. Through the experience on the veld Martha
has an intimation of a different order of reality. Later she has a similar
experience when she and her friend, both pregnant, take off their
clothes and luxuriate in the rich red mud created by a summer rain-
storm. If she had been able to listen to these experiences, the course
of her life might have been different.

Unlike her two marriages, which were detours into the common
emotions and mythologies of her time, Martha's love affair with
Thomas, a Polish Jew, brings spiritual insight. She begins the affair
simply because she is ready for a sexual experience. "All right, then,
not Thomas. But somebody, and it would be soon" (*L*, 60). But

Thomas it is, and the relationship is more than she has bargained for. With Thomas, she experiences a form of transcendence through sex, a kind of communion with a deeper level of self, which she has not experienced with any of the other men in her life. Making love with Thomas, Martha is in the grip of a powerful force she does not understand, a force that produces feelings similar to those she had had on the veld. "No, it was too strong, it was not . . . easy; much easier to live deprived, to be resigned, *to be self-contained*. No, she did not want to be dissolved . . . this experience was something unforeseen, and therefore by definition not entirely desired" (*L*, 99).

Later, after her experiences with Lynda, Martha would understand it. With Thomas she had contacted "great forces as impersonal as thunder or lightning or sunlight or the movement of the oceans being contracted and heaped and rolled in their beds by the moon, swept through [their] bodies . . . being in the grip of this force—or *a* force, one of them. Not sex. Not necessarily. Not unless one chose to make it so" (*FGC*, 496). Sex with Thomas makes Martha conscious of the relation between the violence of the time and her own deepest self. In their lovemaking Martha is painfully aware that Thomas, a Jew, "very nearly had not left Poland" (*L*, 159). The knowledge that Thomas was almost killed by the Nazis makes their relationship more precious to Martha. However, even in what might seem to be Martha's most deeply personal relationship, impersonal violence obtrudes. "When Thomas and she touched each other, in the touch cried out the murdered flesh of the millions of Europe . . . it was all much too painful, and they had to separate" (*L*, 159). Martha becomes conscious of the presence of violence in her deepest self when Thomas tells her he is going to Palestine to fight for Jewish survival. She protests that she does not believe in violence, but recognizes that no one in the twentieth century is innocent.

> Suppose one has loved a man . . . [was] touched by him, but certainly in one's deepest self, and this man . . . murders another out of revenge, what does it mean, saying: I don't believe in violence?
> Having lived through a war when half the human race was engaged in murdering the other half, murdering more vilely, savagely, cruelly, than ever in human history, what

does it mean to say: I don't believe that violence achieves
anything?
. . . Martha was the essence of violence, she had been
conceived, bred, fed, and reared on violence (*L*, 195).

Child of a wounded soldier and the woman who nursed him, Martha
had first married a soldier going off to war and then a political refugee
of war. With Thomas, however, Martha becomes conscious of how
violence had affected her throughout her life. Later she deepens her
knowledge of the region of power and force that their relationship
opened to her and deepens her knowledge of the violent undercurrent
of the times.

In the first four novels of *The Children of Violence*, Martha's
inability to find a self-image causes her to drift through life, motivated by the forces of the time, more than by her deepest self. She has
moments of transcendence and insight, but she is unable to integrate
them. In *The Four-Gated City*, Martha stops drifting and gradually
learns to understand, integrate, and deepen her knowledge of herself
and the times in which she lives.

*The Four-Gated City*—the most complicated novel in the series—
stretches from the early fifties to the late sixties, longer than the time
span of the other four novels together, and has a prophetic afterword
reaching into the nineteen nineties. At the beginning of the novel
Martha has just arrived in London to start a new life. Walking by
the Thames in a moment of illumination, she knows herself as a "soft
dark empty space," a "soft dark receptive intelligence (*FGC*, 38),
a "quiet empty space behind which stood an observing presence"
(*FGC*, 38–39). She knows that this space is the location of insight.
In this space the "watcher" lives, that old friend she later describes
as "that part of me which watches all the time . . . The only part of
me that is real—that's permanent, anyway" (*FGC*, 238). In this space,
"her whole self cleared, lightened, she became alive and light and
aware" (*FGC*, 36). In this space she is alone with herself. "This was
the best thing she had known, to walk down streets interminably . . .
her head cool, watchful, alert, waiting for the coming of the visitor,
silence" (*FGC*, 37). Martha recognizes this moment as being similar
to the moment of insight on the veld. At this moment she values

the experience of clarity, lucidity, knowledge, and insight above all else. Martha's statement that she is alone and had never been otherwise is significant. She recognizes again that the core of her self is alone and independent of the relations and attachments she forms. She wishes she could explore this region further (*FGC*, 37). But she knows that she does not have the strength to get through the dark night of the soul, "when the dark deepened and one thought it would remain, being so strong" (*FGC*, 38). She hears a voice repeating, "Mother, must I go on dancing?" (*FGC*, 40-42) and knows she must live more deeply before she will be able to plumb nonordinary experience further. As she puts it, she had "debts . . . to pay" (*FGC*, 40), she needed to integrate and assimilate areas of her experience before she could brave the night from which illumination would spring. She had lived too quickly, too superficially for too many years. She must slow down, wait, work through the experiences she had already had, but at a deeper level.

Promising herself she would remember the clear-lit space she had just rediscovered, Martha decides against a reasonably well-paying secretarial position, and takes a job, temporarily, as assistant and secretary to Mark Coldridge, an author trying to finish a book. Not having a place to stay, she moves into an empty room in the Coldridge house on Radlett Street and stays there almost twenty years. As if by providence, the house on Radlett Street provides her with the perfect opportunity to reexperience, assimilate, and understand her experience.

Martha's development in the house on Radlett Street follows definite stages. Martha begins to remember the times alone with herself when she has gained insight. She learns to protect her right to those times. She experiences motherhood, and through children broadens and deepens her understanding of herself and the times in which she lives. She pays debts and relives past experiences that she had not integrated or understood. She confronts her mother and understands how she had struggled to create an identity different from her mother's. She experiences depression and confronts a mythology of liberation offered by the culture—psychology—and finds it lacking. She decides to pursue her own inner growth instead of a relationship and thus frees herself from the mythology of sexual love. Finally, she explores the "madness" with her friend and guide, Lynda, and gains visionary powers.

Planning to stay only temporarily in the house on Radlett Street, Martha waits for something to happen. During her period of waiting Sally-Sarah, Mark's sister-in-law, commits suicide, and Martha realizes she must stay on as virtual mother to Francis and Paul, Mark's son and nephew—the last thing she would have expected or chosen. Ironically, she who had walked out on marriage and motherhood spends twenty years mothering other people's children. Yet, oddly, during the years at Radlett Street, Martha grows into a sense of herself that she had been unable to find anywhere else. It is probably significant that Martha experiences motherhood with children not her own. Lessing implies that motherhood can provide opportunities for insight only when the mother has a distance from her children—a situation hard to achieve when the children are one's own. As Barbara Hill Rigney has written, "perhaps disinterested, nonpossessive maternal love is the only kind of love possible in Lessing's world." [5]

Each character who lives or spends time in the house at Radlett Street is marked by the chaos and violence of the times—from Paul, whose Jewish refugee mother committed suicide after her husband, a spy, defected to the Soviet Union to left-wing Patty Samuels, who has a nervous breakdown when Stalin's death revealed the repressiveness of his regime, to Lynda, whose powers are labeled madness by the psychiatrists, to John Patten, whose arrest for homosexuality becomes a cause célèbre. In her position as mother, matron, and counselor, the one who holds everything together, Martha absorbs the experiences of the other characters. At one point Martha describes herself as "a kind of special instrument sensitized to mood and need and state" and feels "herself (or rather the surface of herself) to be a mass of fragments, or facets, or bits of mirror reflecting qualities embodied in other people" (*FGC*, 352). Though she experiences this time as a tremendously exhausting day-to-day struggle in which she must fight to retain her own integrity, in fact the time is one of collection and purgation. As she says:

> How very extraordinary it was, this being middle-aged,
> being the person who ran and managed and kept going . . .

> it was as if more than ever one was forced back into that
> place in oneself where one watched; whereas all around
> the silent watcher were a series of defenses, or subsidiary
> creatures, on guard, always working, engaged with—
> and this was the point—earlier versions of oneself . . .
> (*FGC*, 354).

Through the others she finishes the unfinished struggles of her childhood and young adulthood, heals the old wounds, and, as she puts it,
pays her debts. She emerges stronger, able to cope with almost anything. For Martha, motherhood is a time for gaining insight, for living
in that clear-lit space that is the watcher's. In her role as mother-
counselor, Martha experiences not only the currents of the various
personal lives that she holds together, but, through them, the currents
of their times. This is the basis from which she later develops prophetic
powers.

Another result of Martha's intense concentration on holding
things together in the house is that she begins to "see" and "hear."
She hears the thoughts of Mark and Paul, and she sees a picture of
Dorothy's suicide attempt a week before it happens. When she asks
her psychiatrist, Dr. Lamb, about it, he says that she "imagined"
these things (*FGC*, 324) and implies that she only saw what she was
predisposed to see. This explanation, like his word "déjà vu," tells
nothing. Later in the book Lessing explains that *"what will happen
is a development of what is already happening"* (*FGC*, 554). The
powers Martha begins to develop are a direct result of her intense concentration on the dynamics of the relationships in the house.
The powers Martha develops come from experiencing events more
deeply than the others. Because she experiences on a deeper level,
she knows what will happen. Martha learns that there are currents of
energy she can "plug in" to. Her whole life as mother and counselor
is a process of tuning in to currents of energy or what some might
call the psychological dynamics in the house. That Martha takes
the process a step further than most mothers (or than most mothers
recognize they have taken it) is a result of two special circumstances—
her concentration on the processes of her own inner life and Lynda's
presence, which enables her to talk about and recognize the processes
of her inner life.

However, even though Martha develops special powers as a result of her mother role, she has unfinished business with her own mother. Martha hates her mother because she is repressed and bitter. Mrs. Quest resents Martha because Martha has rejected the sacrificial mother role she had adopted. Martha's relation with her mother was strained to the breaking point because Martha desperately needed a mother she could want to emulate.[6] Because the relation between mother and daughter is central in the formation of woman's image of self, exploring it forces a woman to plumb the deepest levels of her experience.

Thus, Martha's mother's visit forces her to explore regions of herself she has long avoided. Her mother's impending arrival plunges Martha into an incapacitating depression. She becomes familiar with madness, "For, suddenly, far from mental illness (as distinct from neurosis) being something that happened somewhere else, it was all around her ..." (FGC, 227). As Martha relives the painful experiences with her mother she becomes conscious again of the watcher (FGC, 225). During this time she tells Dr. Lamb that the watcher is "the only part [of me] that's real—that's permanent, anyway" (FGC, 238). This realization is very important for Martha because it is a reaffirmation of the pledge she made to herself before she came to Radlett Street, to explore the region of the watcher further. The two women never really communicate with each other during Mrs. Quest's visit. But as she is leaving, Mrs. Quest says to Martha, "I wonder what all that was about really?" and Martha replies, "Yes. So do I" (FGC, 286). For both women, the real work of the visit goes on beneath the surface, where each confronts her image of self.

Just before her mother's arrival, Martha turns to Mark for comfort. "She and Mark made love, remained inside a tender and charming fantasy life where there was no responsibility, no time" (FGC, 245). Yet even within this beautiful space Martha is conscious of the watcher (FGC, 239). Martha begins to feel a conflict between her desire to explore regions of her self alone and her desire to be with Mark. She gets up early in the morning to spend time by herself; she begins to spend her evenings alone as well. Finally she realizes that she not only needs time apart from Mark, but that she needs psychic distance from him as well. For Martha, the psychic independence that Woolf symbolized as "a room of one's own" requires giving up sexual dependence on men. As Sydney Janet Kaplan has noted, Martha fears loss of ego in sexual relationships.[7] "She had to stop being this helpless creature who clung and needed" (*FGC*, 287). A decision to put her relation to her self ahead of her relation to a man is not easy for a woman who has been brought up on the myth of love, a female salvation myth. But it is a decision women must make (at least symbolically) if they are to pursue the interior journey that Martha commits herself to.

Mrs. Quest's visit also pushes Martha into confrontation with psychology, another mythology of salvation available in the culture (another being the Left, which she rejected earlier). Martha looks to her psychiatrist as a kind of savior. Before she had gone to see Dr. Lamb, she had begun working on remembering her past. After she sees him, she finds herself unable to work on her own. He becomes her authority figure, and she depends on him. The therapy sessions drain her energy and leave her lethargic. Finally, she quits therapy and begins to work alone without any external authority.

The significance of Martha's battle with the myth of psychology is symbolized by Lynda, who was destroyed by psychologists who called her powers madness. Later, after her own confrontation with the self-hater, Martha realizes how close she came to losing her mind at the hands of a psychiatrist: "A DOCTOR OR A PSYCHIATRIST WOULD HAVE NEEDED ONLY TO USE THE LANGUAGE OF THE SELF-HATER AND THAT WOULD HAVE BEEN THAT. FINIS, MARTHA! . . . BRING OUT YOUR DRUGS! YES, YES, YOU KNOW BEST, DOCTOR . . ." (*FGC*, 553). On her own, with the knowledge she had gained from Lynda, Martha was able to confront the chaos within her.[8]

After the children are grown and no longer making constant demands, Martha enters another of her waiting periods. "I don't know what it is I'm waiting for—something" (*FGC*, 453). Then Lynda breaks down again and Martha is called upon to stay with her. Her time with Lynda is the most crucial period in Martha's spiritual journey. All her previous experiences can be seen as a preparation for the insight she gains with Lynda as her guide.

At first Martha sees her task as keeping Lynda from falling off the edge.. Then she watches Lynda methodically tap and beat a path around the walls of the room with her hands and her head—until a circle of bloody marks are traced on the wall. The image of Lynda tapping and beating against the walls, one of the most powerful images in the book, captures the fundamental dynamic of Martha's entire journey. Finally, Martha realizes the meaning of Lynda's act. She is not, as Mark thought, trying to escape from the room.

> When she pressed, assessed, gauged those walls, it was the walls of her own mind she was exploring. She was asking: Why can't I get out? What is the thing that holds me in? Why is it so strong *when I can imagine, and indeed half remember, what is outside?* Why is it that inside this room I am half asleep, doped, poisoned, and like a person in a nightmare, screaming for help but no sounds come out of a straining throat? (*FGC,* 494).

As Martha recognizes what the "mad" woman is doing, she recognizes that "she was part of Lynda (*FGC,* 491). Whereas Lynda is attempting to get out of the sickness that incapacitates her, Martha wants to get out of the ordinary way of experiencing that prevents her from reaching the lit space of understanding.

Sitting in the room with Lynda, Martha plugs into the energy Lynda has concentrated for her struggle. "She was being swept by small storms, waves of—what? It was a current that made her limbs want to jerk and dance" (*FGC,* 495). Martha comes to understand that there is a vast impersonal sea of energy in which all are immersed. If, instead of jerking and moving wildly, one waits, the energy will accumulate. Lynda is often tuned into this current of energy, but because she has not had a guide, she has often been overwhelmed by its power. Many people are aware of this reservoir of energy, but, calling it anxiety or tension, they exercise, have sex, drink, or take drugs. Each of these activities can dissipate the energy. Sex can accumulate it, as Martha learned earlier with her lovers Thomas and Jack. Martha recognizes that this vast energy is neutral and can be used for good or ill. "The impersonal sea could become the thousand volts of hate as easily as it could become love—much more easily, human beings being what they are" (*FGC,* 497). With Lynda, Martha comes into contact with the forces that have made the century in which she lives. Contact with the people in the house has prepared her; she is able to understand the currents she discovers.

When Martha lets the energy accumulate she begins to hear thoughts from Lynda's mind, and then she experiences a "great chaos of sound" (*FGC*, 498), which Lynda calls "the sound barrier" (*FGC*, 499).

> . . . and words, shrieks, gunfire, explosions, sentences, came in, faded, or stayed . . . Her whole body, organism, vibrated, shook, was being shattered to bits, by the force with which the sea of sound entered her. Her head was a jar, a bedlam; but, as she was about to cry out, scream, let go of control, perhaps bang her rioting head against the walls, she looked at Lynda . . . and remembered . . . [Lynda] had remarked, "I must get through the sound barrier" (*FGC*, 499).

Martha is terrified by this region of sound that mirrors the violence and chaos of the century. Luckily, she has Lynda's experience to show her how to live through it. Even with Lynda's help, however, Martha thinks "that it was not possible to 'get through' and that she was doomed forever to be shattered by sounds as powerful as pneumatic drills inside her brain" (*FGC*, 500). At this point she is rescued by sleep.

The next morning when Martha walks outside, she has a mystical union with nature much more powerful than the one she had had earlier on the veld. "The sky, oh the sky! and the trees in the square, whose branches moving in the gentle air sent her messages of such joy, such peace, till she cried, Oh trees, I love you, and sky I love you!" (*FGC*, 505). The intense joy produced by the experience sharpens her sense of the insignificance of her ordinary life. ". . . oh, how could I have borne it all these years, all this life, being dead and asleep and not seeing, seeing nothing . . ." (*FGC*, 505). As she continues to walk she sees human beings as "slugs . . . half, uncompleted creatures" (*FGC*, 506), "sleepwalking . . . not aware of themselves, of other people, of what went on around them" (*FGC*, 507). Her judgment is harsh, clearly that of one newly awakened.

Yet Martha does not retain this judgmental attitude when she returns to everyday reality. She senses that the experiences she is having are shared by others. "She knew . . . that if she was feeling something, in this particular way, with the authenticity, the irresistibility, of the growing point, then she was not alone, others were feeling the same . . ." (*FGC,* 512). To confirm her sense that her experiences are shared, Martha reads mystical books from several traditions. She finds that they all speak of the same "processes, the same psychological truths" (*FGC,* 515). They all speak of fear as the primary obstacle to transcendence—"fear of what other people might think; fear of being different; fear of being isolated" (*FGC,* 516). This reading confirms Martha's earlier intuition that Lynda is not mad, her experiences "derived from some finer, or at least more potent, air" (*FGC,* 492).

Martha listens to the region of sound again and finds that its most abiding voice is "an antagonism, a dislike of Martha" (*FGC,* 518). Gradually, Martha comes to realize that this self-hater "was the same as the jeering disliking enemy who—it was clear now—was not personal to Martha, but must be in a lot of people" (*FGC,* 519). At this point Martha recognizes that Lynda's illness stems from her inability to control the self-hater.

Martha's month in the basement with Lynda, exploring regions of nonordinary reality, is a rite of passage. Her earlier apprehensions of another dimension of reality are confirmed. The center of her life shifts decisively as the region of nonordinary reality and the insight it offers become the goal of her quest; it is the city she had dreamed about. It is important to note the sisterhood and sharing between Martha and Lynda. Each is a guide and teacher for the other. Lynda shares with Martha her knowledge of the nonordinary regions, based on her long experience with them. Martha shares with Lynda the strength to cope with ordinary life. It is as if two separated parts of women's experience, mother and witch or madwoman, are joined. From the integration of the separated comes a new power.

Shortly after the experience with Lynda, Martha spends several months alone in a room exploring the regions she had visited with Lynda. Looking into the sound region further, Martha sees the roots of sadism, masochism, anti-Semitism, and all the other hatreds of the time in the deepest regions of her self. This experience confirms the insight she had had with her lover Thomas, that she was the essence of violence. "She would discover herself uttering sloganlike phrases, or feeling emotions, which were the opposite of what she, the sane and rational Martha, believed" (*FGC,* 538). Charting these thoughts and emotions in her own self, Martha recognizes that this "hating . . . *is the underside of all this lovely liberalism"* (*FGC,* 539). Nothing human is alien to her. "*I am what the human race is. I am 'The Germans* [who] *are the mirror and catalyst of Europe' and also: 'Dirty Hun, Filthy Nazi'* " (*FGC,* 539). Struggling with the self-hater, which she calls the Devil, Martha eventually realizes that she is not totally in its power. She can pull herself away from its territory, as she does to go out to dinner with the Coldridges one night. But she also finds that as long as she remains in its territory, she cannot defeat the power of hate, violence, and chaos that she has discovered within herself.

The chaos and violence Martha discovers in herself has also shaped the twentieth century. This current of hatred and violence lies just under the surface, and, as Martha says, all a Hitler has to do is tap it and his power is guaranteed. In confronting chaos and violence within herself, Martha completes her journey of becoming a conscious member of her generation. Most are unconscious of their participation in violence. Martha's conscious appropriation of the currents of the time is the source of her power to prophesy.

It is important to stress that Martha is unable to conquer the hater. Martha finds that when she returns to ordinary life, the voice disappears. It had "become a silly nagging voice . . . And soon, the thing was all over—finished. Her mind was her own" (*FGC,* 556). Martha can conquer the fear that is a large part of the hater's power, and she can learn to acknowledge the self-hater's power without succumbing to it. But she cannot root it out of herself; the hater's power is too deeply entrenched in the violence and chaos of the times. Martha's inability to conquer the hater is a portent of her prophecy of disaster.

At the conclusion of the novel, the house on Radlett Street has been sold and Martha prepares to leave. Once again she has no definite plans. Martha's thoughts about her future sum up the insights she has gained on her journey. "She had learned that one thing, that most important thing, which was that one simply had to go on, take one step after another: this process itself held the keys" (*FGC*, 588). Martha has learned to trust her capacity to grow and learn from any situation. There is no other person, no place outside herself, necessary for the process of insight that she has learned to value above all else.

> Where? What is it? How? What's next? Where is the man or woman who—she would find herself back with herself (*FGC*, 588).

> Where? But *where?* How? Who? No but *where*, where . . . Then silence and the birth of a repetition: *Where?* Here. Here?
> Here, where else, you fool, you poor fool, where else has it been, ever . . . (*FGC*, 591).

Martha has learned that there is no answer to the questions, or rather that the questions always come back to herself and her solitude. It does not matter where she goes or what she does as long as she maintains contact with that inner core of herself, which is the location of her capacity for insight. This core of her self, which she had earlier called the watcher, is the one constant in her life. Her trust in that capacity of her self accounts for her "non-passionate feeling of inner completion."[9]

The appendix at the conclusion of the narrative consists of a series of letters, some from Mark's son, Francis, and some from Martha, which report the disintegration of society. These predictions made in 1968 are haunting. Wiretapping, opening letters, and informal spying "were taken for granted, even approved of" (*FGC*, 602). A national campaign was launched against corruption and decadence (*FGC*, 603). *"Nothing worked"* (*FGC*, 604), and a pointless violence erupted everywhere (*FGC*, 608). "We *were* poisoned" (*FGC*, 612), by traffic and aircraft noise, by foul air, by drugs, preservatives, toxic substances used on crops, atomic wastes dumped in the sea (*FGC*, 612). All of these things were intimations of the catastrophe that finally occurred in 1977 when poison from radioactive missiles leaked in the North Sea.

After she leaves Radlett Street, Martha takes care of children on communes in the country and Lynda finds a psychoanalyst who is interested in her powers. Lynda and Martha make contact with others who have powers similar to their own, and they begin to imagine that people with such powers can make a dent in the repressive political and social structures of the time. Lynda and the others begin having a form of consciousness that must be developed through discipline.

Before the catastrophe, Martha escapes to an island. There she cares for "special children," many of whom have been born with the power to see or hear, a power that Martha developed only after long struggle. Those who can hear tune in to the "noises of terror and misery that are so loud now" (*FGC,* 645) and refuse to "understand" that such things are part of human nature. They do not hurt each other or fight. There are also seven "new children" who seem to have been born with "the knowledge of what the human race is in this century" (*FGC,* 647). "It is as if—can I put it like this?—they are beings who include this history in themselves and who have transcended it" (*FGC,* 647). One of the children says that some day all the human race will be like them.

The appendix concludes enigmatically and ironically with a note to Francis concerning one of the "new children." The child is classed as subnormal, fit only for work on a vegetable farm (*FGC,* 649). The final letter states that he is to become a park and garden inspector, perhaps an allusion to the gardeners who were the guardians in Martha's vision of the four-gated city. Lessing hints that these special children may bring the new age of harmony into existence— or perhaps they will be destroyed by a society that does not understand their powers.

The prophecy in the appendix follows two lines. One extends the negative tendencies of the century into disaster. The other extends the positive tendencies into hope for a future that transcends the disaster. Both reflect the fact that what will happen is a result of what already is happening.

Looking at Martha's quest in its entirety, we see that her spiritual consciousness is defined by the "watcher," the part of herself that observes, understands, becomes conscious of the deeper dimensions of her experience. The watcher has a less aggressive relation to reality than ordinary male consciousness, but it is not passive. When she describes the watcher as a soft, dark, receptive intelligence, Martha does not mean it is merely a passive receptacle. The watcher is an active consciousness. Far from being undifferentiated passivity, it is a form of consciousness that must be developed through discipline. Waiting is the major discipline of this consciousness. Waiting is not a passive activity; Martha waits with purposefulness. She does not know what she is waiting for, but when it is given to her, she takes active steps to explore it. Thus she discovers Lynda's territory in one of her waiting periods and explores it further on her own.

Martha's knowledge of self and world is always concrete. She uses books only to verify her insights, to confirm something she knows or half knows. Her knowledge is not abstract, nor unconnected to ordinary life. Nothing she knows is arbitrary, surprising, or unrelated to something she had known before. Her self-knowledge and knowledge of the world are intimately related.

Martha feels part of a process that transcends her conscious control. Since she is not concerned to change the process or herself, but only to understand, she desires nothing in particular. She trusts that whatever happens, wherever she goes, the process of living will provide her with opportunities to deepen her insight.

An observing, connected, deepened consciousness is the source of Martha's prophetic power. As she understands what is happening in her self, in the children, and in the world in which she lives, she comes to understand what will happen as a development of what already is happening. This form of prophecy is organic, not exoteric, an insight into processes everyone is involved in, not revelation from an external source. The prophetic powers that Martha and Lynda develop are similar to the powers of the medial woman described by Toni Wolff.[10] The archetypal medial woman is "immersed in the psychic atmosphere of her period, but above all in the collective (impersonal) unconscious." She constellates "what is in the atmosphere and just beginning to find expression." Wolff notes that a strong positive identity is necessary for the medial woman so she can "discriminate what is personal from what is impersonal"; otherwise the medial woman will be swamped by the objective psyche and become an agent of chaos and destruction. Wolff's theory illumines the destructive nature of what Martha calls the region of sound and explains Lynda's initial inability to use her powers because she developed them before she had attained a strong positive identity. The totality of Martha's experience of ordinary life was necessary before she could discriminate, and help Lynda discriminate, between her personal self and the currents of the times.

Martha's quest, though firmly rooted in women's experience, also reflects Lessing's fascination with Sufi insights. As has been noted, *The Four-Gated City* can be understood as a long Sufi teaching story that may assist "an interior movement of the mind." A number of Martha's insights reflect Sufi teachings. For example, Sufis believe that enlightenment comes through experience, not intellect, and urge the individual to assume responsibility for her own life, not to trust any authorities, not even spiritual teachers. Sufis believe that conventional or "logical" ways of thinking must be transcended if insight is to be gained. And Sufis believe that hope for survival of the human race is to be found in evolutionary change in which new organs will be developed. These organs will enable humans to transcend time and space through telepathy, prophecy, and clairvoyance. They believe this evolutionary process can be aided by the exercise of these capacities among individuals who are now living. Finally, the Sufi way is neither active in the political sense, nor passive in the classical mystical sense.[11]

Because women have not created philosophies, have rarely had access to spiritual authority, and rarely have had the opportunity to pursue exclusively intellectual or spiritual paths, it makes sense that they might be attracted to the practical, antiauthoritarian elements of the Sufi path. Their roles as women and mothers encourage in them a receptivity that opens them to mystical insight and even telepathic or prophetic power. Though I find the Sufi notion of developing new organs interesting, I do not find it a satisfying resolution of the spiritual quest/social quest dilemma. It seems to me a solution too much rooted in conventional messianism, in the hope for salvation from outside the human situation.

Though Martha's journey strikes a responsive chord in many women, Lessing's view of the relation between the spiritual and social quest is disturbing. Like Martha, Lessing seems to believe that nuclear catastrophe is inevitable. And this apocalyptic vision leaves her pessimistic about social change and somewhat detached from women's social quest for equality in relationships, work, and politics. There are many days when I find Lessing's pessimism compelling and can easily envision the nuclear accident she describes. I always find her depiction of Martha's observing, connected, deep powers of insight and prophecy powerful. And I even believe that the development of psychic powers may be one weapon the individual has against the megamachine of the modern corporate and state power. However, I want women to be more than witnesses and prophets of disaster or hope, more than mothers or nurturers of "new children." I believe it is possible that women's new naming of self and world can stem the tide of violence and disintegration Lessing so convincingly depicts. I find more to hope for in the new naming that emerges from the sisterhood of women than in Lessing's vision of the miraculous "new children."

# 6. Homesick for a Woman, for Ourselves: Adrienne Rich

ACCORDING to two of her most important critics, "from the beginning [Adrienne] Rich's theme, personal and collective, has been woman in the patriarchy: her own identity, the identity of woman on man's established terms; and, more and more urgently, the possibility of identity on her own, on woman's own terms."[1] While much of Rich's poetry has centered on the subjective realm of personal relationships, she has recognized the connection between the personal and the political: "there is no private life which is not determined by a wider public life," reads the epigram to *Diving into the Wreck* (*DW*, 2).[2]

Women's relationships take place within a world that has been defined for centuries by men and that only recently is beginning to be defined by women. In Rich's vision, women's relationships with men reveal men's inability to feel, their fascination with power and control, while women's relationships with women reveal the energy that can transform a culture of power and death into a culture of life and rebirth. That Rich's recent poetry has a political dimension has been obvious to serious readers of her poems—both to those who have found Rich's politics annoying and distracting and to those who have found this element enlightening and exhilarating.[3] That Rich's poems also have a spiritual dimension has been less clearly recognized.

75

Adrienne Rich's understanding of woman in the patriarchy and woman's quest for identity on her own terms has followed parallel courses with that of Mary Daly, her close personal friend. According to Daly, feminism is not simply a political and social movement (though it most certainly is that), it is also a spiritual journey that begins in an *experience of nothingness,* a shattering of the conventional pieties that had supported the self, comparable to the mystic's dark night of the soul. When supported by the *courage to see,* the clear-sighted facing of the emptiness at the heart of conventional views of the self, it leads to an ontological insight, a *new seeing* or revelation of "what is," which then requires a *new naming* of self and world.

The experience of nothingness and the courage to see are at the heart of the poems in *Diving into the Wreck.* The "wreck" into which the poet dives is the dark underside of marriage and politics in the patriarchal world. Beneath the myths of civility, love, and power wielded to protect, Rich discovers a landscape of terror. Emotional distance and control turn to violence in men; self-effacement smolders into consuming rage in women. For Rich, "personal problems" with men become emblematic of a destructive lack of concern for life and growth characteristic of the world men have shaped.

To describe the wreck she finds, Rich uses extreme language. No *"conservateur"* of present reality,[4] Rich imagines apocalyptic destruction that will bring purification: she speaks of "testing bombs" (*DW,* 3), of fire "feeding on everything" (*DW,* 47), of "ice . . . forming over the earth" (*DW,* 11). While sharing the apocalyptist's penchant for purifying fire and ice, Rich's vision is particularly feminist. The fire she imagines is fueled by the anger of women who have suppressed themselves for too long. The apocalypse that she envisions may be the inner transformation of women whose anger consumes their ties to the patriarchal world rather than an external destruction.

In order to face the nothingness at the heart of patriarchal marriage and politics, Rich had to give up many of the myths that had shaped the lives of women of her generation—"whole LP collections, films we starred in / playing in the neighborhoods . . . the language of love-letters, of suicide notes" (*DW,* 3)—a whole romantic fantasy in which women's lives were defined entirely by their relationships (or lack thereof) to men. Giving up these fantasies required the courage to see. In Rich's poetry, revelation is expressed in imagery of visionary seeing. She speaks of lying "awake under scarred plaster" (*DW*, 11), of "another eye" that opens "underneath my lids" (*DW*, 17), of "waking first" "in a house wrapped in sleep" (*DW*, 20). The poet's acute vision enables her not only to see the wreck, but also to imagine ways to transcend it. Rich thus begins to speak of "diving down" beneath the culture and its values and of going back into history in search of a healing vision.

In the first poem in *Diving into the Wreck*, "Trying to Talk with a Man," Rich writes of nothingness in a relationship with a man. Trying to talk with him is like "testing bombs," the landscape they inhabit is a "desert" with "deformed cliffs" filled with "dull green succulents," images of destruction and ugliness (*DW*, 3). Though they are "surrounded by a silence" (*DW*, 3), the man does not even realize that there is a problem in communication. To him the desert is no metaphor, and he talks idly of the adventures of people who are stranded in such locales. Though unable to touch the poet emotionally, he nonetheless communicates a will to dominate, a "dry heat" that "feels like power" (*DW*, 4), his emotionless conversation filling the space in which she might venture to speak. Recognizing the futility of trying to talk with him, the poet feels "more helpless with you than without you" (*DW*, 3), realizing, perhaps for the first time, that the feared state of being a woman without a man might be easier than the frustration of living with one whose life runs on a different course from her own. Though helpless with the man, the poet begins to value herself, in particular the sensitivity he lacks. Her own "acute angle of understanding" appears to her as "an underground river" and a "locus of the sun," the only signs of life and renewal in an otherwise desolate place (*DW*, 3).

In "When We Dead Awaken," Rich continues to explore the wreck. Images of failed relationships, "stones . . . souvenirs of what I once described / as happiness" (*DW*, 5) are juxtaposed with images of senseless destruction in war, "guerillas are advancing / through mine-fields" and urban decay, "trash / burning endlessly in the dump" (*DW*, 5). The poet now begins to connect the personal and the political:

the emotional insensitivity men display in relationships is also reflected in their insensitivity to human suffering in foreign wars and in city ghettos. Like Doris Lessing, Rich suggests that women's intense focus on the personal life provides them with insights into the forces that operate in public life.

As in the previous poem, Rich places hope in the creative vision of women, choosing an image from women's traditional work. She imagines women "working with me to remake / this trailing knitted thing, this cloth of darkness, / this woman's garment, trying to save the skein" (*DW*, 5). Though the image recalls women's traditional role of knitting clothes for her family, Rich transforms it. The image suggests that women can disentangle themselves from the darkness of patriarchal culture and create a new culture out of the threads they hold. Women have always, Rich suggests, worked with what is at hand, delicately separating that which is salvageable in order to create something needed, something beautiful, like a knitted sweater that protects against cold yet is decorated with patterns and colors. Rich's reference to women's traditional arts here and elsewhere in her poetry is not a sentimental evocation of women as conservators of culture. On the contrary, Rich's feminism enables her to view traditional women in a new light. Excluded from the center of male-created culture with its power politics, wars, and great "art," women unself-consciously weave the threads of an alternative cultural vision. Though in the past women's works served only to humanize the periphery of male culture but not to transform it—to bind the wounds but not to stop the war—Rich recognizes women's traditional work as the creation of an alternative cultural vision. The threads of nurturing, emotional sensitivity, and simple beauty may be woven by women of today into a new culture. In recognizing a continuity between herself and the numberless women whose names were never in history books, Rich finds strength to believe that it is possible to weave a new culture—not from scratch, but from threads our foremothers have left us.

In the next stanza of the same poem, Rich elaborates the image of women's power apart from men. She identifies herself with an old chest with "a huge lock shaped like a woman's head / but the key has not been found" (*DW*, 6). Suggesting that women's minds have been locked up in patriarchy and their insights lost to human culture, Rich vows to reclaim the lost treasure of women's understanding. She "give[s] up keeping track of anniversaries" (*DW*, 6), memorials to time and space shaped by women's relationships to men, and "begin[s] to write in [her] diaries more honestly than ever" (*DW*, 6) in order to get in touch with her own, woman's, thoughts and feelings. In the final stanza of the poem Rich suggests that the ability to see and name the wreck is a source of power. Speaking out of "the matrix of need and anger" women speak of nothingness, name "unmeaning– / yet never have . . . been closer to the truth / of the lies we are living" (*DW*, 6). Though it is painful, the truth is freeing. Women's vision is a life force in the midst of nonlife: "the faithfulness I can imagine," Rich writes, "would be a weed / flowering in tar, a blue energy piercing / the massed atoms of a bedrock of disbelief" (*DW*, 6). Women represent life pushing up from under, small and scraggly at first, but with the potential to move blacktop, to transform death into life.

The tremendous power that is unleashed when women have the courage to see the nothingness of male-defined culture and relationships is further explored in other poems in *Diving into the Wreck*. As her vision enables her to see the wreck more and more clearly, Rich turns increasingly to apocalyptic imagery. In "The Phenomenology of Anger," she meditates on things that are about to burst into flames—"a pile of rags the machinist wiped his hands on" (*DW*, 27), the mowed hay during a heat wave (*DW*, 27). The poet imagines herself egging the fire on, "huddled fugitive / in the warm sweet simmer of the hay / muttering: *Come.*" Rich imagines women's anger as a purifying fire that will consume the faceless unrestrained male violence that gunned down babies in My Lai and that visits itself on women in more restrained form in the bedroom. In another poem, "The Ninth Symphony of Beethoven Understood At Last As a Sexual Message," Rich meditates on the masculine nature of violence, which filled the newspapers during the Vietnam war. In that poem Rich suggests that male power when disconnected from the day-to-day involvement in home and family life egotistically asserts itself without regard for others. Beethoven's "isolated soul / yelling at Joy from the tunnel of the ego" (*DW*, 43) is not unrelated to corporate executives in America "masturbating

/ in the factory / of facts" (*DW*, 28) in "Phenomenology." In the latter poem Rich in a horrifying image juxtaposes men's inability to express feelings in relationships with women to men's apparent lack of feelings for the lives they destroy in war. "I suddenly see the world / as no longer viable: / you are out there burning the crops / with some new sublimate / This morning you left the bed / we still share" (*DW*, 29). Even more graphically, "Last night, in this same room, weeping / I asked you: *what are you feeling? / do you feel anything? /* Now in the torsion of your body / as you defoliate the fields we lived from / I have your answer" (*DW*, 29). For Rich the man in her bed whose feelings are locked inside himself, whose body lies rigid and contorted as she weeps, is emblematic of that kind of male emotional distance and control that can tolerate the violence of the Vietnam war, the defoliation of crops, and the killing of the babies of women.

As she explores the anatomy of her relationships with men, Rich comes to a conclusion that is shared by many women who have lived all their lives with men: " 'The only real love I have ever felt was for children and other women. / Everything else was lust, pity, / self-hatred, pity, lust' " (*DW*, 30). Mary Daly's term "the courage to see" seems especially appropriate here. Women's lives have been so shaped by the expectations expressed in the stories of men that women have often not even experienced their own experience. As the woman in "Dialogue" says, *"I do not know / who I was when I did those things / or who I said I was / or whether I willed to feel / what I read about"* (*DW*, 21). Because the experience of nothingness is so deep for women within a culture defined by men, Rich imagines an apocalyptic solution as her escape. "Night after night / awake in prison, my mind / licked at the mattress like a flame / till the cellblock went roaring" (*DW*, 31). This image of fiery destruction is repeated in other poems in *Diving*. The poet views herself as "wood, with a gift for burning" (*DW*, 20), in one poem, and in another describes her mind "burning as if it could go on / burning itself, burning down / feeding on everything / till there is nothing in life / that has not fed that fire" (*DW*, 47).

While images of liberation through fiery destruction are frequent elsewhere in the volume, in "Diving into the Wreck" Rich imagines herself as an undersea diver exploring a wrecked ship in order to "see the damage that was done / and the treasures that prevail" (*DW*, 23). As other images in the poem make clear, the poet's undersea exploration is metaphor for an interior journey to the source of her inner power, "I have to learn alone / to turn my body without force / in the deep element" (*DW*, 23), and for a quest to find a mythic prehistory when women were revered. Though having read "the book of myths" (*DW*, 22), the poet is keenly aware that even stories of ancient times are told from a male perspective: the book of myths that she carries is one "in which / our names do not appear" (*DW*, 24). She is seeking the primal source, "the wreck and not the story of the wreck / the thing itself and not the myth" (*DW*, 23). The revelation that arrests her in this poem is the androgyne.

> This is the place.
> And I am here, the mermaid whose dark hair
> streams black, the merman in his armored body
> We circle silently
> about the wreck
> we dive into the hold
> I am she: I am he (*DW*, 24).

That she is speaking of a revelation is clearly indicated in her words and imagery. The undersea exploration is a pilgrimage; the diver enters the waters of transformation and rebirth, and her stark announcement "This is the place" indicates that she has reached the sacred center. For Rich the androgyne represents a buried treasure, a centering vision of wholeness that might enable women and men to move beyond the deformed symbiosis of male power and female submission.[5]

The title of Rich's most recent book of poems, *The Dream of a Common Language,* suggests that Rich is turning from describing the wreck of male culture to the new naming of self and world that arises out of the experience of nothingness. The title calls attention to the key role of language in articulating and shaping women's experiences of new being. In this book, Rich also turns from dissecting male/female relationships and the disasters of male culture to a more clearly chosen identification with and focus on women. Though there are still some poems about men, there are more and more about women—poems about women scientists, artists, mountain climbers who dared to define new roles for women, twenty-one poems written to a woman lover, and new poems about the ordinary women, mothers and homemakers whose nurturing values provide a counterpoint to patriarchal values.

Since few things are as upsetting to many men and some women as a woman who defines herself apart from men, it seems important to discuss briefly the significance of Rich's identification with women and her lesbianism. In the last poem in *The Dream of a Common Language,* Rich names "the homesickness for a woman, for ourselves" (*DCL,* 75),[6] which is the inspiration of much of her recent poetry. In another section of the same poem she writes, "Birth stripped our birthright from us, / tore us from a woman, from women, from ourselves / so early on" (*DCL,* 75). In *Of Woman Born* Rich states that few women in this culture feel "mothered enough."[7] To understand these statements, we must recall that in a patriarchal culture where men are the storytellers, women learn early on that men are more important than women. Men's relationships to each other are celebrated, and almost the only stories about women are about women's relationships to sons, husbands, brothers, male lovers. Because of this, the mother-daughter relationship, which might be one of the most celebrated of all human relationships, and which Rich celebrates in *Of Woman Born* as "resonant with charges ... the flow of energy between two biologically alike bodies, one of which has lain in amniotic bliss inside the other, one of which has labored to give birth to the other"[8] is fraught with ambivalence. The mother may prefer sons who will grow up to be valued in patriarchy, and she may fear that her daughter's talents could make her unacceptable to men. She may even attempt to keep her daughter from becoming too smart, strong, or independent. She will probably teach her daughter that men are more valued than women and that the only route to power and acceptability for a woman is through relationship to a man. As the daughter senses her mother's ambivalence toward her and learns of society's devaluation of her mother and other women, her feelings toward her mother will also become ambivalent and she too may learn to prefer men in all things. The cost of this ambivalence for mother and daughter is great. For in denying each other and preferring the male, each is denying herself as well. When Rich says "Birth stripped our birthright from us," she means that as birth tears women from their mothers' bodies, so it also is the point where women begin to learn that they are not valued. As soon as she leaves the womb a girl child is faced with the ambivalence of her mother and other women and men toward women, toward herself. Instead of the mothering or nurturing she might receive from a woman, one like herself, she is never really loved and encouraged to become all she can become. "Homesickness for a woman" thus refers to feelings of being unnurtured as a little girl, which continue throughout a woman's life. *The Dream of a Common Language* celebrates the beginning of the reversal of that age-old pattern of female ambivalence toward women. It celebrates the beginning of a new era in which women will be nurtured by other women and nurture themselves.

For Rich, loving women can be expressed in many forms—as mothers, daughters, sisters, friends, colleagues, and lovers. For women who are lesbians, Rich's poems about lesbian relationships are important on the literal level, for they tell a woman's story that has rarely been told. Moreover, Rich believes that lesbianism is a logical outgrowth of loving women. But it is also important to remember the symbolic dimension of Rich's love for women. On that level, even her most explicitly sexual poems can speak to all women (and even to men) of the difficulty and the joy of learning to honor, respect, and nurture women, and to love oneself as a woman.

In addition, the poems in *Dream* are important to all women who understand the need to define themselves out of their own experience. Naming their experiences of power and meaning outside their relationships to men does not necessarily (though in some cases it may) mean that women will eschew all relationships with men. What it does mean is that, for the first time in recorded history, significant groups of women feel the need to live and see and name reality without regard for what men say.

Rich's concern with creating a new language to express women's visions of wholeness and power is reflected in her rejection of words, patterns, and images she had once used. The androgyne, a central image in the poems in *Diving into the Wreck,* is now rejected by Rich as not adequately expressive of the new being of women. In "Natural Resources," a poem in which she describes the energy women have wasted searching for "The phantom of the man-who-would-understand, / the lost brother, the twin—" (*DCL,* 62), Rich concludes that man has required "women's blood for life / a woman's breast to lay its nightmare on" (*DCL,* 63). Using women as a refuge, men have created a world in which violence and war are the norm. Men are "children picking up guns / for that is what it means to be a man" (*DCL,* 63) or else they display "a passivity we mistake / —in the desperation of our search— / for gentleness" (*DCL,* 63). Rich's vision of men may not reflect the totality of men's experience of themselves or even of women's experience of the men they know as *exceptional* men—as Rich acknowledges when she says, "I am tired of faintheartedness / their having to be *exceptional* / to do what an ordinary woman / does in the course of things" (*DCL,* 64). Nonetheless, the picture she presents reflects all too clearly the experience of many women with many men.

Because she identifies men with the violence of their world, Rich declares:

> There are words I cannot choose again:
> *humanism androgyny*
>
> Such words have no shame in them, no diffidence
> before the raging stoic grandmothers (*DCL,* 66).

Androgyny implies that women accept what men have been as part of the wholeness they seek. This Rich can no longer accept. Increasingly, Rich sees more to admire in the resilient creative energy of women than in the union of or transcendence of male and female. The raging stoic grandmothers are the uncelebrated heroines who have endured and attempted to repair the wounds the violence and insensitivity of patriarchal culture have created. They have created the human bonds in a culture of death.

If women reject the imagery of transcendence devised by males, then women must create a new language and imagery to express their visions of wholeness and power. The enormity of this task cannot be overstated. In "Origins and History of Consciousness,"[9] the poem from which the title *The Dream of a Common Language* is taken, Rich confronts the nothingness from which new creation must come in "the whiteness of the wall" and, "contemplating last and late / the true nature of poetry" (*DCL,* 7), realizes the burden of responsibility the poet bears. The white wall symbolizes the poet's mind after it has been stripped of the tradition of language and imagery that she now knows as patriarchal. Facing genuine emptiness, the poet asks herself why poetry is written and discovers that it arises from "the drive / to connect. The dream of a common language" (*DCL,* 7). While she may have heard similar words before, the dream of a common language takes on new meaning for the poet who has now consciously isolated herself from the protection of men and male traditions of poetry. Only out of deep isolation does the poet realize what it means to say that the calling of the poet is to create connections through language. She will create a language in which women's connections to each other are named and celebrated, a language that may transform the patterns of violence and domination perpetrated by the language of men.

The notion of creating connections between women through poetry is further explored in "Transcendental Etude," the concluding poem of *Dream.* Like "Origins," this poem describes the experience of nothingness Rich feels, "the pitch of utter loneliness / where she herself and all creation / seem equally dispersed, weightless, her being a cry / to which no echo comes or can ever come" (*DCL,* 75). The survivors of this experience, Rich says, learn to speak "new language" (*DCL,* 75).

The key theme in this new language is the celebration of women's experience, women's values, and women's history. Rich celebrates women through four kinds of images. She writes of extraordinary women who have defied patriarchy's strictures to create new kinds of lives for women—Elvira Shatayev, a Russian mountain climber; Marie Curie, discoverer of radiation; Paula Becker, painter; and Clara West-hoff, sculptor. She remembers the ordinary women—mothers, daughters, and grandmothers—the nurturers of life in an often violent society. She celebrates women lovers, creating new values through their choice of women. And finally she speaks of the woman alone, the woman who has chosen, not solitude, but the possibility of solitude, in choosing to be who she is—a woman no longer desperate for the love of others because she loves herself. In weaving these four images of women together, Rich has created a tapestry richer than any of the four apart. She suggests that what these women have in common is more important than how they differ. She finds in each an image of a particular kind of female strength. Shatayev and the stoic grandmother, the lesbian lover and the mother covering a sleeping child are no longer the polar opposites as in patriarchal language and vision. All share a common love of life and beauty, a common revulsion for the sufferings inflicted on humankind in war and other power plays.

In "Phantasia for Elvira Shatayev" Rich imagines the words that might have been spoken by the leader of a women's climbing team that perished in the attempt to climb Lenin Peak in August 1974. Rich celebrates the strength of women who dared to stretch their bodies and their minds to limits women have never dared before. Rich's imagination was captivated by the spirit of sisterhood that must have been displayed by this group of women who chose to climb without men—with each other.[10] Rich imagines that the women experienced the "yes" of their own inner strength growing as they prepared for the climb. "What we were to learn     was simply     what we had / up here     as out of all words     that  *yes*  gathered / its forces" (*DCL*, 4). "Out of all words" refers on the literal level to the women conserving their breath in the thin air of the high mountain, but on the symbolic level it refers to their journey to a space where patriarchal civilization has not penetrated, where its words are without meaning. In this space the individual "yes" of each woman fuses together into a common strength greater than any of the women could have imagined. As Shatayev might have described it:

> . . . *I have never seen*
> *my own forces so taken up and shared*
> *and given back* (*DCL*, 5).

In the end the women perish in a freak storm, but Rich believes the story of their strength and determination will enter into the shared consciousness of women.

> When you have buried us     told your story
> ours does not end we     stream
> into the unfinished     the unbegun
> the possible (*DCL*, 5).

Rich imagines that as the women's bodies decompose on the mountaintop, even the mountain is transformed by their energy: "this mountain   which has taken   the imprint of our minds / through changes elemental and minute" (*DCL*, 5). Changes in the face of the mountain are emblematic of the change the stories of these women will make in the minds of women, which after all are easier to transform than stone. For this reason Rich asserts that "every breath     and gasp   and further foothold / [of these women] is somewhere     still enacted   and continuing" (*DCL*, 5).

The second image of woman celebrated in *Dream* is the ordinary woman—mother, daughter, grandmother—who through the ages has nurtured life. This celebration of traditional female values surfaced in *Diving into the Wreck,* in the image of women reknitting a tattered garment, "trying to save the skein." In "Natural Resources" Rich elaborates the image of women weaving, suggesting that the strength of the "raging stoic grandmothers" is one that can be tapped by today's women who are seeking to re-create the world. Comparing the world to a tattered blanket, Rich pictures women's traditional contribution to civilization:

> this fraying blanket with its ancient stains
> we pull across the sick child's shoulder
>
> or wrap around the senseless legs
> of the hero trained to kill (*DCL*, 66).

Women's work of nurturing and binding wounds is deliberately contrasted with men's work of going to war. Even Rich's choice of the word "hero" is deliberate, suggesting that war is not only men's duty but something they glory in. Rich urges today's women to complete the work of their grandmothers:

> This weaving, ragged because incomplete
> we turn our hands to, interrupted

> over and over, handed down
> unfinished, found in the drawer
>
> of an old dresser in the barn,
> her vanished pride and care
>
> still urging us, urging on
> our work . . .
> to help the earth deliver (*DCL*, 67).

In this image Rich connects women's traditional values to contemporary feminist values. Rich urges women today to pick up the thread of their grandmothers' values—to weave, not garments, but a whole new civilization; to deliver, not babies, but new vision. The connection between traditional women and the poet is not just the metaphoric—and some might say abstract—connection of weaving and delivering. The connection is one of values. Rich urges women to pattern their actions after their grandmothers' values, not after the values of men. She urges women today to treasure in themselves not the heroic gesture of the great man, but "a universe of humble things" (*DCL*, 66), the everyday faithfulness of countless women before them.

In the final poem in *Dream*, Rich sees a woman's creation of a small collage from "bits of yarn, calico and velvet scraps" as "the rock-shelf further / forming underneath everything that grows" (*DCL*, 77). The tradition of female values reflected in this collage will be the foundation for the transformation of culture. Such a woman Rich observes, "quietly walked away / from the argument and jargon in a room" (*DCL*, 76). Like the female mountain climbers who ventured beyond patriarchal civilization and discovered a new language, or the lesbian lovers whose space is defined by female presence, women of the past, with much less fanfare—without anyone even noticing—also chose to live outside the culture defined by the "argument" and "jargon" of men. Such a woman was not heroic in the ordinary sense; she had "no mere will to mastery, / only care for the many-lived, unending / forms in which she finds herself" (*DCL*, 77). In contrast to the world of argument and jargon that she has left, this woman lives in reverence for *life* in its minutest detail, in awareness of the simple beauty of *things* known to one who spends her days in ordinary domestic tasks. The materials for her creation include "small rainbow-colored shells /

sent in cotton-wool from somewhere far away, / and skeins of milk-weed from the nearest meadow / . . . the darkblue petal of the petunia, / . . . not forgotten either, the shedsilver / whisker of the cat" (*DCL,* 76). These objects are not found in museums, this artistry not recorded in books. But Rich's carefully detailed description of this woman's materials makes the reader see with new eyes the important human value, the reverence for life and things, expressed in her art. If life were organized around "such a woman's" values, Rich seems to be suggesting, civilized men would not bomb cities and villages, de-stroying ordinary people and the things they hold dear.

A third, and in many ways central, image in Rich's celebration of women is found in her poems exploring love between women. The images of nurturing and respect for separateness in these poems con-trast with the images of emotional distance and power plays in the poems in *Diving.* For Rich, women's love for women has cosmic sig-nificance because it overturns ancient patriarchal patterns in which women nuture but are not nurtured, in which women are rarely loved fully and unequivocally *in their strength* as well as in their weak-ness by either women or men. As we have seen, the poems in *Dream* are inspired by a "drive to connect," which Rich later names "a home-sickness for a woman, for ourselves." For Rich the vision (though not always the reality) of full, deep, emotional sexual love between women is not the only, but may be the most complete, expression of love for "women, for ourselves." In "Transcendental Etude" Rich writes movingly of that primordial desire for the mother that men fulfill in their love for women, but which in women usually remains unfulfilled:

for that acute joy at the shadow her head and arms
cast on a wall, her heavy or slender
thighs on which we lay, flesh against flesh,
eyes steady on the face of love; smell of her milk, her sweat (*DCL*, 75).

The longing for the mother (which Dorothy Dinnerstein also movingly describes in *The Mermaid and the Minotaur*) is the root of women's longing to be touched by a woman and is fulfilled in a lesbian relation-ship.

But loving a woman is more than a return to the arms of the mother. In "Splittings," a poem in which Rich fights with her reservoir of primordial pain, she addresses this point directly. She admits, "I want to crawl into her for refuge    lay my head / in the space    between her breast and shoulder / abnegating power for love" (*DCL,* 11). But she rejects that pattern explicitly and says, "I choose to love    this time    for once / with all my intelligence" (*DCL,* 11). To love with intelligence is contrasted with loving out of infantile need and affirms both lover and beloved as separate adult persons.

In her love for women, Rich affirms both her age and her body. Though aging is not affirmed in our culture, older men are often considered attractive by younger women, while older women are ignored or ridiculed. Thus Rich's affirmation of her aging is an important reversal of a cultural pattern. In the third of "Twenty-One Love Poems," Rich muses on the feeling of youth that being in love creates, and thinks, "Did I ever walk the morning streets at twenty, / my limbs streaming with a purer joy?" (*DCL,* 26). But she contrasts that feeling with her awareness of time, "At twenty, yes: we thought we'd live forever. / At forty-five, I want to know even our limits" (*DCL,* 26). Rich not only accepts age, but treasures the more realistic perspective experience brings.

In "The Floating Poem, Unnumbered," Rich affirms the ecstasy of sexual passion of the body. Like the unnumbered card of the Fool in the Tarot deck, Rich's unnumbered poem reflects aspects of experience that cannot be neatly categorized. Sexual ecstasy gives humans a taste of perfect pleasure only to drop them back into the mundane world. In the unnumbered poem, Rich celebrates her lover's body and her own and affirms sexual passion as an intimation of eternity when she says, at the end of the poem, "Whatever happens, this is" (*DCL,* 32). She speaks of her lover's "tender, delicate" touch and her "traveled, generous thighs," affirming the specialness of a woman who like herself has been schooled in tenderness, yet whose legs are heavy and show signs of age. Perhaps the most beautiful image in the poem is Rich's naming of her own vagina as a "rose-wet cave" (*DCL,* 32). This image invites women to think of vaginas as delicately colored and sweet smelling, and to compare the discovery of the beauty of their vaginas with the awe and delight of an explorer who, entering a crevice in a rock, discovers a pink-walled cavern with a hidden spring. Comparing the vagina to a cave is also a reminder of the ancient mythologies in which Goddesses were worshiped in caves because of their structural similarity to women's wombs.

In Rich's poems about relationships with women, as in her poems about relationships with men, the personal is emblematic of the political. Rich contrasts the world she knows with her lover to the larger world in which they both live. In the first lines of "Twenty-One Love Poems," Rich describes the city's violence and decay, "Wherever in this city, screens flicker / with pornography, with science-fiction vampires, / victimized hirelings bending to the lash, / we also have to walk . . . / through the rainsoaked garbage, the tabloid cruelties / of our own neighborhoods" (*DCL,* 25). In a desolate cityscape Rich views the women lovers as "the red begonia perilously flashing / from a tenement windowsill" or "sycamores blazing through the sulfuric air, / dappled with scars, still exuberantly budding" (*DCL*, 25). With images reminiscent of the underground river in the desert and the weed flowering in tar from *Diving*, Rich envisions women's love as the source of hope, beauty, and tenacious life in an otherwise barren place.

Contrasts between the love of women and the violence of the city sometimes overwhelms Rich. In the fourth love poem, the poet is upset by an old man who lets an elevator door slam against her grocery-laden arms and then mutters "hysterical" when she protests his cruelty. Then in her apartment she opens the mail to read of the sadistic genital mutilation and torture of a male political prisoner who writes, "*You know, I think that men love wars . . .*" (*DCL*, 27). These confrontations with male violence—one minor, but direct; the other major, but indirect—bring tears of outrage to the poet's eyes as she moans, "and they still control the world, and you are not in my arms" (*DCL*, 27).

At times Rich sees the contrast between the world of male violence and the world of women's love as a vision of hope. In the sixth love poem, Rich ponders her lover's "small hands, precisely equal to my own—" (*DCL,* 27) and imagines a world controlled by hands such as theirs. "In these hands, / I could trust the world" (*DCL*, 27-28), she writes, suggesting that women would manage the world with a concern for life and things. The images in this poem recall those in the chapter in *Of Woman Born* where Rich contrasts the "hands of flesh" of the midwife with the "hands of iron" of medical gynecologists. Rich marvels at the skill of midwives, and while not discounting the importance of the invention of the forceps (a metal tool developed by a man to aid in the removal of the baby in a difficult birth), she ponders its symbolic significance. Why did the use of the forceps become routine medical practice for normal births? Is there in men a fear or aversion to women and the life force that makes male doctors want to distance themselves from birth with a metal tool?[11] In this poem about her lover's hands, Rich imagines that women would handle power differently than men. Her juxtaposition of images is telling. She imagines women "handling power tools or steering wheel" *and* "touching a human face" or turning "the unborn child rightways in the birth canal" (*DCL*, 28). Technology and hands of flesh—hands of flesh guiding technology. Rich also imagines a woman piloting a *rescue* ship through icebergs or mending a broken Greek cup. Again the images show woman's delicate touch and concern for life and things. The cup pictures "ecstatic women striding / to the sibyl's den or the Eleusinian cave" (*DCL*, 28), an image that reminds women of their roles as priestesses and prophetesses in the ancient mysteries of birth and death. Rich believes the hands of women, unlike those of men

> . . . might carry out an unavoidable violence
> with such restraint, with such a grasp
> of the range and limits of violence
> that violence ever after would be obsolete (*DCL*, 28).

If taken as a *description* of what women in power inevitably do, it is naive. But as a vision of how culture *might* be transformed by women who *consciously* remember the heritage of traditional female values, the image is less easily dismissed. There may be more substance in Rich's vision of women transforming culture than in the hope that men in power will somehow reverse the pattern of centuries and put human values first.

Eventually the relationship described in "Twenty-One Love Poems" fails, in part because of the scars and open wounds the two women carry. Rich sees her lover as a woman "drowning in secrets, fear wound round her throat" (*DCL*, 35), whose past suffering makes her turn away from intimacy. Rich's solitary meditations about the end of the relationship are included in several of the last of the "Twenty-One Love Poems." In these poems Rich looks at the fourth image of woman—the woman alone—and affirms her own solitude and her decision to live her life openly, honestly, and with risk. Though living alone is difficult for women who have been schooled in the importance of relationships, solitude is likely to be a part of every woman's life—especially the lives of women who challenge society's norms.

In the fifteenth love poem, Rich ponders the circumstances that contributed to ending the relationship and concludes, "If I cling to circumstances I could feel / not responsible. Only she who says / she did not choose, is the loser in the end" (*DCL*, 33). In accepting responsibility for what happened, Rich feels less a victim and is able to view her solitude more positively. In the seventeenth poem Rich refuses to take comfort in the notion that theirs was a tragically doomed relationship. Instead she looks clearly at what happened and rather than blaming herself, the other woman, or fate, measures the various factors:

> this we were, this is how we tried to love,
> and these are the forces they had ranged against us,
> and these are the forces we had ranged within us,
> within us and against us, against us and within us (*DCL*, 34).

Here Rich omits the particular in favor of the universal in a chant-like litany. By focusing on the common elements in her story, she is able to accept what happened without feeling either personally victimized or personally guilty. The refrain, "within us and against us, against us and within us," allows Rich to acknowledge that it is difficult for all lovers, especially women lovers, to love in this society, and to accept a degree of personal responsibility (but not guilt) for the failure of her love affair.

By the last love poem, Rich has come to terms with her grief and anger (*DCL*, 34) and imagines her mind as a ritual space like Stonehenge, where insights come to her like a "cleft of light" (*DCL*, 35), the moon, rising over ancient stones. The image suggests peacefulness and calm, a place where dispassionate reckonings with *what is* can take place. Rich states that this is a place where "solitude, / shared, could be chosen without loneliness" (*DCL*, 35). Since she mentions no one else as physically present, Rich affirms a connection with readers who recognize similar spaces in their own minds. She differentiates between loneliness that cries out for company and the solitude in which silence and lack of distraction are savored for the insights they call up from deep within. To live with solitude is not easy, Rich says, but one can carefully stake out the space, clearing the mind of the extraneous, so that what remains is essential: "the circle," image of the clearing in the mind; "the heavy shadows," reminders of all that is arrayed within us and against us; "the great light," the place in the mind where all is understood as part of patterns larger than the self and accepted without sorrow, regret, or desire. "I choose to be a figure in that light" (*DCL*, 36), Rich says, accepting herself simply as she is. She describes herself as "half-blotted by darkness, something moving / across that space, the color of stone / greeting the moon, yet more than stone: a woman." Here Rich affirms the eternal patterns in her movements. As a figure in the light, she is the ancient seeker of understanding. But she also chooses to be not just human, not just a seeker, but a woman.[12] As if to reaffirm her choice to be a woman seeker of wisdom, and to underline the solemnity of her creative task, Rich concludes the poem by repeating, "I choose to walk here. And to draw this circle" (*DCL*, 36). Strikingly, the final poem in the love-poem cycle is Rich's poem to herself and her solitude. Here Rich acknowledges that through loving a woman she has learned to love herself. She has learned, as she says in "Transcendental Etude," to *"love myself– / as only a woman can love me"* (*DCL,* 76).

Besides reflecting the structure of a woman's spiritual quest, especially the new naming of self and reality, the "Twenty-One Love Poems" contain many subtle references to a symbol system that will be recognized by those familiar with the women's spirituality movement. Many women have found in the Tarot cards a prepatriarchal set of images that can be more useful in charting their spiritual journeys than Biblical symbolism.[13] The "Twenty-One Love Poems," plus one floating poem, mirror the twenty-one plus one major archana (or archetypal images) of the Tarot deck. Moreover, the poems allude to the archetypal symbolism of the Tarot deck. The twenty-first archana is the World, a card that according to feminist interpreter Z. Budapest represents "the dance of life," "affixing your name to creations," and is a "very creative space."[14] This corresponds to the twenty-first poem, in which Rich ponders her life, gains insight, and assumes responsibility for who she is. The fifteenth card, the Devil, represents "bondage and ignorance,"[15] and it is in this poem that Rich toys with the idea of blaming circumstances for the failure of her relationship. The fourth card is the Emperor, which according to some feminist interpretations means patriarchal power, and in the fourth poem Rich describes the intrusion of the man in the elevator and the tortured prisoner. The third archana is the Empress, who reflects "Venus-Aphrodite, Lady of plenty . . . [who] brings love relationships."[16] Rich's third poem celebrates love. The list could go on, but the point seems clear: Rich has consciously chosen the form of the Tarot cards as the space in which to organize her feelings and insights. This choice is significant because it shows that Rich accepts the terms in which the womanspirit movement is redefining spirituality. The references to her vagina as a cave and to her mind as Stonehenge are further allusions to women's spirituality. This, of course, should not be surprising to those who recall Rich's evocation of prepatriarchal "matrifocal" societies in *Of Woman Born.*

Adrienne Rich's poetry in *Diving into the Wreck* and *The Dream of a Common Language* reflects a spiritual journey that begins in an experience of the nothingness of her relationships with men and the values of male culture and proceeds to a new seeing, a new being, and a new naming of self and ultimate value. As a poet Rich is particularly conscious of the role of language in articulating the new vision of what is. The new being and the new naming come to the fore as Rich celebrates the strength of women, the power of female values, and the importance of women's love for each other and for themselves.

Weaving together the various strengths that shape women's heritage—the courage and daring of extraordinary women like Elvira

Shatayev who challenged patriarchal denials of women's strength, the nurturing of life and care for things that ordinary women display every day, and the new feminist vision of women loving women—Rich creates a tapestry of female vision that points toward a transformation of culture. To imagine a woman with Elvira Shatayev's courage to challenge patriarchy, who cares for people and things not for the kind of power that comes from dominating others, and who loves other women and herself (whether sexually or not) as only a woman can love a woman, is to begin to see that image of a woman who is a person Martha Quest sought. To imagine thousands of such women is to begin to understand how the world might be transformed by women's new naming. Of the women writers discussed in this book, Adrienne Rich provides the clearest vision of the path toward the integration of spiritual vision into social reality. Though all women will not follow the path Rich has charted, her visions of women's strengths, women's values, and women's love for women, for themselves, holds much to inspire all women's quests.

# 7. "i found god in myself . . . & i loved her fiercely": Ntozake Shange

A GUTSY, down-to-earth poet, Ntozake Shange gives voice to the ordinary experiences of Black women in frank, simple, vivid language, telling the colored girl's story in her own speech patterns. Shange's gift is an uncanny ability to bring the experience of being Black and a woman to life. Those who hear or read her choreopoem *for colored girls who have considered suicide/when the rainbow is enuf* may feel overwhelmed by so much reality, so much pain, so much resiliency, so much life force. They may even feel they have actually lived through the stories they have heard.

Like Adrienne Rich, Shange is acutely aware of the nothingness experienced by women in a society defined by men. But Shange is also aware of a double burden of pain and negation suffered by women who are Black in a society defined by *white* men—where Black women are not even granted the ambivalent recognition some white women receive for youth and beauty or for being wives and mothers of white men. Shange's poem also reflects the double strength Black women have had to muster to survive in a world where neither being Black nor being a woman is valued.

Though Shange's forte is the vivid re-creation of experience, *for colored girls* is more than the simple telling of the Black girl's story. It is also a search for the meaning of the nothingness experienced and a quest for new being. In Shange's poems the experience of nothingness is born of the double burden of being Black and a woman, but the stories she tells bring a shock of recognition to every woman who has given too much of herself to a man.[1] The heart of the experience of nothingness in *for colored girls* is a woman's loss and debasement of self for love of a man. But what makes Shange's poems more than just another version of *Lady Sings the Blues*—a theme of sorrow and survival too familiar to Black women (and white women)—is Shange's refusal to accept the Black woman's sorrow as a simple and ultimate fact of life. She probes for a new image of the Black woman that will make the old images of the colored girl obsolete. Shange envisions Black women "born again" on the far side of nothingness with a new image of Black womanhood that will enable them to acknowledge their history while moving beyond it to "the ends of their own rainbows."

*For colored girls* began as a series of separate poems, but as it developed Shange came to view "these twenty-odd poems as a single statement, a choreopoem."[2] In the stage production six actresses dressed in the colors of the rainbow—yellow, red, green, purple, blue, orange—and one dressed in the brown of earth and warm-toned skin alternately speak the twenty-odd poems, each a story. While one speaks the others listen attentively or mime the story, their interest creating a sense of sisterhood and sharing. Often a story told by one woman evokes sympathetic "yeahs," or the telling of a related story, or even dancing from the other women. In a sense the dialogical form of Shange's play re-creates the consciousness-raising group of the women's movement, where in sharing experiences and stories, women learn to value themselves, to recognize stagnant and destructive patterns in their lives, to name their strengths, and to begin to take responsibility for their lives. The sense of dialogue in Shange's choreopoem is an invitation to the women in the audience to tell their stories. What emerges is a tapestry of experiences, interwoven with a sense of plurality and commonality.

The title of the choreopoem provokes questions. Why did Shange use the outdated term "colored," which Black people abandoned as oppressive in the sixties? How is the rainbow enough? And what does a rainbow have to do with suicide? In a television interview, Shange explained why she used "colored girls" in the title of her poem. She spoke of the importance of Black self-definition, of taking pride in dark skin and African heritage. She said that her own name, "Ntozake," is an African name she chose as a way of affirming her African roots. But, she said, it was also important to affirm her American ancestors. She recalled that her grandmother's last words to her were that she was a precious "little colored girl." Thinking about this made Shange realize that "colored" was not only a term used by whites to define Blacks, but also a term of endearment in the Black community. To reclaim the name "colored girl" was to reclaim her relationship to her grandmother, a part of her story. The juxtaposition of "colored girl" with "rainbow" enables Black women to see the varied tones of their skin as a reflection of the glorious hues of the rainbow, not as a color to be borne in shame. And, though colored girls have considered suicide because they have been abused by white society and Black men, this need no longer be the case. "The rainbow" is now understood as an image of their own beauty, and it "is enuf."

Shange further explained the meaning of the enigmatic last line of her title, when she said, "One day I was driving home after a class, and I saw a huge rainbow over Oakland. I realized that women could survive if we decide that we have as much right and as much purpose for being here as the air and mountains do."[3] Here Shange describes a kind of mystical insight—being does not require justification, it just is. Within the poem, Shange restates the last line of the title, "but are movin to the ends of their own rainbows" (64). This restatement extends the mystical insight further: after recognizing their grounding in being, Black women must begin to create their own reality, for example, by creating symbols like the rainbow to express their infinite beauty.

*For colored girls* begins with a poem spoken by the lady in brown about the importance of naming and celebrating experience in song and story:

> sing a black girl's song
> bring her out
> to know herself

> to know you
> but sing her rhythms
> carin / struggle / hard times
> sing her song of life
> she's been dead so long
> closed in silence so long
> she doesn't know the sound
> of her own voice
> her infinite beauty (4).

Shange recognizes that without story the self is diminished: the Black woman is "half-notes scattered // without rhythm / no tune" (3), "interrupted solos // unseen performances" (4).[4] Without celebration of her unique possibilities, the Black woman wonders if she is fully human, "are we ghouls? // children of horror? // the joke?" (4). The Black woman teeters on the edge of madness, "i can't hear anythin but maddening screams" (4). Because she has no sense of her own worth and is desperate to find someone to affirm her value, she trusts too much in men, and when they disappoint her, she laments, "& you promised me // you promised me . . ." (4). If only she knew "the sound // of her own voice // her infinite beauty" (4), she might not be so gullible, so unrealistically dependent on men. The lady in brown concludes the poem with a statement of Shange's purpose in writing *for colored girls:*

> sing the song of her possibilities
> sing a righteous gospel
> the makin of a melody
> let her be born
> let her be born
> & handled warmly (5).

Only when her song is sung, her story told, will the Black woman know her potential. She will be "born" as a human being for the first time, because she will be aware of herself as a person with value and a range of choices. As the lady in brown finishes these lines, she is joined by the other six women, who collectively affirm their common purpose: to tell the story of "colored girls who have considered suicide // but moved to the ends of their own rainbows" (6).

In order to sing a colored girl's song, Shange must re-create the language of her experience, a language which, in its concrete particularity, has almost never been spoken. Black women's voices have been negated by the standard (white) English grammar that has forced Black people to fit their experiences into alien language patterns. Black women's experiences have also been negated by a literary tradition that celebrates the experiences of white men. Shange ignores standard grammar in her effort to capture the nuances of Black women's speech patterns and experience. The following lines spoken by the lady in yellow are characteristic of Shange's style:

> it was graduation nite & i waz the only virgin in the crowd
> bobby mills martin jerome & sammy yates eddie jones & randi
> all cousins
> all the prettiest niggers in this factory town
> carried me out wit em
> in a deep black buick
> smellin of thunderbird & ladies in heat
> . . .
> all mercer county graduated the same nite
>      cosmetology secretarial pre-college autoshop & business
> all us movin from mama to what ever waz out there (7).

The idiom of this Black girl's life is reflected in speech patterns, choice of words, details of description, spelling, and punctuation (or rather lack of it). The lack of punctuation and capitalization may reflect Shange's perception of the particularities of Black women's speech and experience. Virginia Woolf once remarked that the translation of women's speech into writing would require the introduction of a new sentence. Women's experience, she said (and here we might add, the experience of all who lack power), does not fit neatly into the rhythms of dominant and subordinate clauses that were patterned after the ordered and hierarchical world of upper-class (white) men.[5] In her own writing Woolf explored a stream-of-consciousness style, which she felt expressed women's experience more fully than the standard sentence. Like Shange's poetic lines, Woolf's sentences lacked precise beginnings and endings and patterns of subordination. (This is also true to some extent of Atwood's and Lessing's prose styles.) In both Woolf's and Shange's writing, experience is perceived as a flow, with pauses, but

without the clear ordering required by the standard sentence and para-
graph. In Shange's poetry the almost complete absence of periods and
capital letters makes this flowing effect even more obvious. Shange
and Woolf would probably argue (and I would agree) that their writing
styles more directly reflect experience as lived and that the order expressed by the standard sentence is an imposition, an attempt to
control reality. It may also be that those who lack power experience
life differently than those who have it or that women experience the
flow of life more fully than men. However that may be, Shange's poems
also reflect her notion that Black speech is close to music, an understanding expressed in the mixed genre choreopoem in which music,
dance, and spoken word are woven together.[6]

Shange is deeply aware that her choreopoem reflects not only
Black, but female experience. In an ironic essay in *nappy edges* entitled,
"wow . . . yr just like a man!" Shange describes how her references to
women's experience are perceived by the (in this case, Black) male
poetic community:

> so anyway they were poets/ & this guy well he liked this
> woman's work/ cuz it wazn't 'personal'/ I mean a man can
> get personal in his work when he talks politics or bout his
> dad/ but women start alla this foolishness bout their bodies
> & blood & kids & what's really goin on at home/ well &
> that aint poetry/ that's goo-ey gaw/ female stuff.[7]

Faced with a double cultural standard that considers the particularities
of male experience universal, but the particularities of female experience too trivial to merit poetic expression, Shange determines to
make her poems even more female oriented:

> i've decided to wear my ovaries on my sleeve/ raise my
> poems on my milk/ & count my days by the flow of my
> mensis/ the men who were poets were aghast/ they fled
> the scene in fear of becoming unclean.[8]

This determination to make her poems reflect female experience and
bodies is evident in all the poems in *for colored girls,* but especially
in those poems that consider abortion, rape, and relationships between
Black women and Black men. For Shange it is important to affirm her

Black woman's body, and this too is reflected in many of the poems. As Shange says, "with dance I discovered my body more intimately than I had imagined possible. With the acceptance of the ethnicity of my thighs & backside, came a clearer understanding of my voice as a woman & as a poet" (xi).

Just as it is necessary to consider the meaning of Rich's lesbian poetry for all women, it is important to understand the significance of a Black girl's song for all women. Each of the three times I saw *for colored girls* performed on Broadway, and each of the many times I have read the poems or heard them on my stereo, I have felt chills up and down my white woman's spine—shocks of recognition that tell me that something deep within me has been unlocked as I hear my experience voiced. Lines like "lemme love you just like i am / a colored girl / i'm finally bein // real / no longer symmetrical & impervious to pain" (44) speak forcefully to many women. Other women can substitute "six feet tall and smart" (as I do) or "with curly Jewish hair" or any of the myriad ways they have been told they fail to live up to the ideal of female attractiveness. It is also not only colored girls who have pretended to be "symmetrical and impervious to pain," who have denied their needs and feelings in order to keep a man. Through the particularities of a Black woman's story, Shange touches a core of pain and self-negation shared by most women. The Black woman's experience of nothingness may be more intense, but it is not entirely different from that of many women whose skin is a more acceptable hue.

The poems in *for colored girls,* when taken as a whole, describe a spiritual journey through the particularities of a Black woman's experience. In this journey an alternation of joy, despair, and reconstitution of self proceeds circularly, musically, rather than linearly. Shange's women move through hope, defeat, and rebirth in several of the poem sequences, until in the last the lady in red experiences a crescendo of despair that leads to a dramatic rebirth of self and a more certain awareness of the self's grounding in larger powers of life and being. The poems in *for colored girls* celebrate the Black woman's life force and capacity for love. They confront her defeat and celebrate her resilience. They provide her with alternatives to the image of the

Black woman as either helpless and defeated, a "sorry" colored girl, or as strong and resilient, "impervious to pain."[9] As one of the women in *for colored girls* admits, the new image of Black womanhood is difficult to imagine, for "bein alive & bein a woman & bein colored is a metaphysical // dilemma / i haven't conquered yet" (45). In her search for new images, the Black woman cannot simply adapt images from the white man, the Black man, or the white woman, because none of these images of being human reflect the fullness of her humanity, the affirmation of both her color and her sex. To search for new images of self is to ask anew the old questions: What is it to be human? Do we need relationships? Sex? What is the relation between body and soul? Shange seeks answers to these questions as she explores the Black woman's experience in her poems.

The first several poems in *for colored girls* create a mood of youthful optimism, playfulness, and joy in being alive. The serious note of the opening poem is interrupted by the singing of the childhood song, "mama's little baby," the reciting of a playful rhyme, and a game of tag. This lighter note, which carries over into the next two poems, expresses Shange's perception that the Black girl's childhood does not always prepare her for the struggles and hard times of her adult experience. As Shange said, "*for colored girls* . . . is a record of me once I left my mother's house. I was raised as if everything was all right. And in fact, once I got out of my house, everything was *not* all right."[10]

"Graduation nite," previously discussed in part, tells the story of a girl's first sexual initiation. While the girl's lower class and sometimes violent environment ("bobby whispered i shd go wit him / fore they go ta cuttin") is evident in her tale, the story is a positive one. Graduation was an exuberant rite of passage for her, and she sang inside: "WE WAZ GROWN    WE WAZ FINALLY GROWN" (9). And later "in the backseat of that ol buick // . . . by daybreak // i just cdnt stop grinnin" (10). The other women join in her memories, dancing and singing "Stay," a song by the popular rock group the Dells.

The following poem, "now I love somebody more than," tells the story of the lady in blue's teen-age fascination with the Caribbean rhythms of Puerto Rican musician Willie Colon. Though this poem too has its serious moments, including a reference to Black self-hatred and color caste systems, "my papa thot he was puerto rican & we wda been // cept we waz just reglar niggahs wit hints of spanish" (11), the poem as a whole is joyous. Beginning with the first "ola" (11), and moving through vivid descriptions of her dancing, "i waz twirlin hippin givin much quik feet" (12), the poem is an invocation to the spirit of music and dance that has brought so much joy to a colored girl's life. The lady concludes with a wild, humorous poem to music, "& poem is my thank-you for music // & i love you more than poem // . . . more than celia lobes cuba or graciela loves el son // more than the flamingoes shoo-do-n-doo-wah love bein pretty" (13).

In white culture the Black woman's sensuality and sexuality have been viewed negatively. Black women have been viewed as sexually loose, as having animallike passions, as willing whores. These images of the white man's imagination have been used to justify sexual abuse and rape of Black women by white men. Despite these stereotypes Shange has chosen to begin her choreopoem with a celebration of Black women's sexuality and love for music and dance. In doing so, she affirms the body and its rhythms of sensuality and sexuality and rejects those white male images of humanity that denigrate the body and sexuality.

While the first two poems celebrate Black women's life force, the next poem, "no assistance," tells of their abuse. The lady in red tells how she loved a man who didn't appreciate her. "I have loved you assiduously for 8 months 2 wks & a day // i have been stood up four times" (13). She "left 7 packages on yr doorstep // forty poems 2 plants & 3 handmade notecards i left // town so i could send to you" (13-14). But his response was to "call at 3:00 in the mornin on weekdays // so i cd drive 27 1/2 miles across the bay before i go to work" (14). Many women may recognize themselves in this woman whose love and creative energy flowed into a man who didn't reciprocate. Some might ask why a woman would allow herself to be treated so badly, and the answer would be that women often believe they have no identity or value apart from men. What makes the story of the lady in red more than the age-old female complaint about abuse by men is humor, anger, and insight. The lady in red mocks herself, saying, "this waz an experiment // to see how selfish i cd be // ... if i waz capable of debasin my self for the love of another // if i cd stand not bein wanted // when i wanted to be wanted // & i cannot" (14). Seeing her actions with humor creates a distance from pain and allows her to express her anger and to take responsibility for ending the affair. "This note is attached to a plant // i've been waterin since the day i met you // you may water it // yr damn self" (14), she says. Because she sees herself as responsible for letting herself be abused, she sees her power to refuse to be a victim (in Atwood's terms). The anger expressed in her last words to this man is the anger of a woman who has realized she doesn't need to waste her time on a man who doesn't value her. Her story calls up feelings of pain and outrage that such an obviously creative and funny woman has not been able to find a man to appreciate and love her.

The lady in orange (played by Shange in the original cast) hears the pain in the lady in red's story and begins to question the poet's calling. If poetry re-creates such pain, then "i dont wanna write," she says, "i wanna sing make you dance ... scream" (14). At that point the whole troupe breaks into dancing with her, and the lady in yellow admits, "we gotta dance to keep from cryin" (15). But the women also urge the lady in orange to continue to speak and finally she does, saying, "i'm a poet // who writes in english // come to share worlds witchu" (16). Thus she affirms her intention to go on writing poems even though they call up pain.

The next two poems speak of painful violations of women's bodies in rape and hack abortion. All the women speak the rape poem together, affirming that unfortunately this is not an individual story. The poem begins, "a friend is hard to press charges against" (17), and continues as several of the women come forward with clichés likely to be spoken by police or others who dismiss a woman's cry of rape. "If you know him // you must have wanted it," they say, or "you know // these things happen ... had you been drinkin" (17). The women angrily retort that unless the rapist is a sex maniac or a stranger, no one will believe them, "pressin charges will be as hard // as keepin yr legs closed // while five fools try to run a train on you" (18). Using gang rape as a metaphor for pressing charges describes

the raped woman's sense of double violation and humiliation—first
by the rapist, then by the criminal justice system. A final humiliation
is that friends can be rapists; women are often "betrayed by men who
know us" (19), and "we cd even have em over for dinner // & get
raped in our own houses" (21). The picture created by Shange's poem
is brutal but true.[11] The stark simple lines of the poem and their
harsh rhythm contrast effectively with the mood of joy expressed
in the first two poems and deepen the feelings of pain and outrage
that were introduced in "no assistance." Shange creates a mood, preparing the audience to experience ever deeper nothingness in a Black
woman's story.

In "abortion cycle #1" Shange re-creates a woman's terror during
an illegal abortion. The poem begins cryptically as four of the women
shriek "eyes," "mice," "womb," "nobody," evoking a feeling of
terror. The rest of the poem, spoken by the lady in blue, is a collage
of images of pain, disgust, fear, shame. "Tubes tables white washed
windows // grime from age wiped over once // legs spread // anxious"
(22). The woman sees dirt and metal instruments; starkly absent is
a kind word, a smile, someone to hold her hand. The images become
more brutal, the feeling of disgust grows, "metal horses gnawin my
womb // dead mice fall from my mouth /" (22). These images capture
the feeling of violation, the pain of an abortion without anesthesia: it
felt like something huge and powerful was inside her womb, like
death was coming out of all her orifices. The woman is hysterical;
she can't cope, "get offa me alla this blood // bones shattered like soft
ice cream cones" (22). Finally the woman explains that she sought
the abortion because she wasn't married, and "i cdnt have people //
lookin at me // pregnant" (22). Her shame dissolves into pain as she
cries inside, "this hurts // this hurts me" (22). At the end of the poem
her feelings of isolation and shame return, as she concludes, "& nobody
came // cuz nobody knew // once i was pregnant & shamed of myself"
(23). This woman's secret shame recalls the opening poem, where it
was stated that as long as the Black woman's story is not told, she
will hear nothing but "maddening screams // & the soft strains of
death" (4). In sharing her story, the lady in blue can begin to break
out of her isolation.

In the next several poems, "sechita," "toussaint," and "one,"

Shange turns the audience to three individual stories which, while not without their own painful dimensions, are not as devastating as the stories of rape and back-room abortion. Sechita dances in the dust of the tent of a tawdry carnival, and though she moves with an elegance that recalls "quadroon balls" (23) or Egyptian Goddesses "performin the rites" (25), her talent and beauty are not appreciated by redneck audiences. Sechita's story tells of the degradation of a Black woman's sexuality and creativity and of her defiance of those who degrade her: "they were aimin coins tween her // thighs / sechita / egypt / goddess / harmony / kicked viciously // thru the nite / catchin stars tween her toes" (25). Refusing to let herself be debased by the dirt and vulgarity of the men who come to see her, she envisions herself as a Goddess and expresses her contempt with vicious kicks of her legs.

In "toussaint," the mood lightens considerably as the lady in brown tells the story of a little Black girl who discovers a book about Toussaint L'Ouverture, the liberator of Haiti. Told in childish speech patterns, the poem touchingly re-creates the world of summer library contests for "who colored child can read // 15 books in three weeks" (26). Elated to progress beyond stories of "pioneer girls & magic rabbits // and big city white boys" (26) to her first story of a "blk man a negro like my mama say // who refused to be a slave" (26), the little girl is disqualified from the reading contest because the book on Toussaint comes from the adult reading room. At the end of the story the little girl exchanges her secret fantasy lover, Toussaint L'Ouverture, for Toussaint Jones, a tough little boy who boasts "i dont take no stuff from no white folks" (30). This poem captures an important dynamic of a young girl's imagination. A Black man's story is certainly more inspiring to a little colored girl than one about big-city white boys, and yet even this story teaches her to put her hopes in men as her savior. Like Martha Quest, and many other women, this little girl believes that the man standing before her is like the man of her dreams. Even though this story ends on a positive note, it shows how a little girl's fantasies prepare her for disappointments with men.

"One," told by the lady in red, is the story of "the passion flower of southwest los angeles" (31), a lady in heat dressed in "orange butterflies & aqua sequins" and out to entice "every man who waznt lame white or noddin out" (31). The passion flower is a woman whose apparent power over men arouses "the wrath // of women in windows" (32), all those women who wait helplessly for the man who never comes. Shange lavishly describes this woman's craft and beauty— "her stomach out // lined with small iridescent feathers" and the "pastel ivy drawn on her shoulders" (32). But she sees beneath the glitter and glamour, a woman not really in control of men or her own life. Despite her bravado, the passion flower really wants to be loved and appreciated, not to chalk men up as conquests. In the second half of the poem, the lady in red describes the passion flower after her seduction is completed. She rises and bathes in "dark musk oil egyptian crystals" (33). And "layin in water // she became herself // ordinary // brown braided woman // with big legs and full lips" (34). And though the lady in red describes with humor the way the mere sight of her as a "reglar colored girl" banished the lover of the night from her bed, no amount of humor can gloss over the pain this woman felt as she "cried herself to sleep" (35). The painful irony in this poem is that this woman's power to conjure men vanishes with the water in her bathtub. Waters that purify and cleanse, so that "she became herself" (34), return her to being a sorry colored girl. Men flee when they see her as she really is. This experience of the inadequacy of her own self and her own body is shared by all women who feel ugly and undesirable without make-up, who curl or straighten their hair, diet or squeeze their bodies into girdles, and feel they must always be dressed in the latest fashions. Black women experience this sense of inadequacy even more deeply than white women, because the ideal of beauty is always white, usually blond, never with nappy hair. So while Shange admires the passion flower's sense of style as expressed in her costume and even in her bath salts, and respects her ability to give men a dose of their own medicine, she also recognizes that the passion flower's power is illusory until she can also be loved as she is, a "reglar colored girl."

The alternation of naming Black women's strengths and naming their abuse and suffering continues in the next poem, "i useta live in the world." In this poem Shange contrasts the universe of free Africa with its "waters ancient from accra / tunis // cleansin me / feedin me"

(36) with Harlem where "my ankles are covered in grey filth // from the puddle neath the hydrant" (36). Black women in Harlem not only live in poverty and filth but also suffer verbal and physical abuse from men who assuage their shattered egos by abusing women. "NO MAN YA CANT GO WIT ME / I DONT EVEN // KNOW YOU // NO I DONT WANNA KISS YOU / YOU AINT BUT 12 YRS OLD" (37), she screams. The ultimate degradation she suffers is the knowledge that she must become violent like her surroundings if she is to survive: "i cant be nice to nobody // nice is such a rip-off . . . is just a set-up" (38-39).

The next poem, "pyramid," considers women's complicity in their oppression. Prior to this poem, the poems in *for colored girls* have considered Black women's abuse by forces outside themselves—rapists, hack abortionists, white rednecks, poverty bred of racism, and men who don't appreciate them. "Pyramid" concerns three friends whose closeness is expressed as "one laugh // one music // one flowered shawl // knotted on each neck" (39), and who allow themselves to be split up by a man. It is an old story of women considering men more important than their friendships with each other. In this case, the women betray a close bond between each other for a man who doesn't even care about any of them. He conquers one, then goes after the other two, who resist his advances at first and then succumb. Finally the first one finds "the rose // she left by his pillow // . . . on her friends desk" (41). When the two women go to confront him, they find him with yet another woman. Shange concludes the poem with the two women comforting each other:

> she held her head on her lap
> the lap of her sisters soakin up tears
> each understandin how much love stood between them
> how much love between them
> love between them
> love like sisters (42).

The play on "between" in these lines brilliantly captures the paradox of these women's friendship. Though they let love for a man *come between* them, the love that *flows between* them, a bond created from shared experience and suffering, reasserts itself. The strongest love between them is their love for each other. Like Rich, Shange celebrates the bond of sisterhood between women as a more reliable source of support than romantic fantasies about men.

In the next series of poems, "no more love poems" #1, #2, #3, and #4, which form the reflective introspective center of the choreopoem, Shange explores the experience of nothingness created by women's dependence on men. In what to me is the most profound poem in *for colored girls*, the lady in orange (originally played by Shange) sings a "requiem for myself / cuz i // have died in a real way" (43). The death she suffered was caused by self-denial and self-deception. "Ever since i realized there waz someone callt // a colored girl," the poem begins, "an evil woman a bitch or a nag // i been tryin not to be that" (42). She wants to give Black men something better, so "i brought you what joy i found" (42). But her treating him gently does not bring a different end to the story; the man still "put my heart in the bottom of // [his] shoe" (43). Her experiences force the lady in orange to face being the woman whose image has been so vilified, the sorry colored girl. As she finally admits, "i dont know anymore / how // to avoid my own face wet wit my tears cuz i had convinced // myself that colored girls had no right to sorrow / & i lived // & loved that way & kept sorrow on the curb / allegedly // for you / but i know i did it for myself // i cdnt stand it // i cdnt stand bein sorry & colored at the same time // it's so redundant in the modern world" (43). In these lines Shange expresses an understanding of why women take abuse from men without complaining: it is just too painful to admit that men have the upper hand in many relationships and that they abuse the women who love them. The young Black girl who knows that she will suffer on account of her race often tries to deny that she will also suffer on account of her sex. However, to begin to admit the depth of her pain and experience of nothingness is the beginning of the road to self-acceptance for every woman.

In the next poem, the lady in purple experiments with being open and honest about her pain. Instead of hiding she lays herself open and says to a man, "i really am colored & really sad sometimes & you hurt me" (44). In accepting herself as she really is, the lady also accepts her particular mind and body. "Here is what i have," she says, "poems / big thighs / lil tits / & // so much love" (44). Though this statement sounds simple, it is contrary to the socialization women receive—never to reveal how smart or creative they are for fear of threatening a man, always to try to disguise the ways their bodies fail to meet the ideal, and never to admit their need for love. The lady in orange has learned to love herself and to be open and honest about her own needs, but her personal growth does not bring her a man of equal caliber. Her cry becomes almost hysterical as she begs for the love she feels she deserves, "please please / this is for you // i want you to love me / let me love you . . . just like i am / a colored girl / i'm finally bein // real / no longer symmetrical & impervious to pain" (44). Here Shange expresses a real dilemma of the strong Black woman, of all strong women: their honesty, openness, and ability to admit vulnerability does not insure that someone will love them; often it only makes them more threatening to men who expect to have the upper hand.

Thus, the lady in blue wonders whether it is worth it to be open and vulnerable if this only leads to a deeper experience of nothingness. She ponders alternatives: "we deal wit emotion too much // so why dont we go ahead & be white then // & make everythin dry & abstract wit no rhythm & no // reelin for sheer sensual pleasure" (44). To her the ideal of the rational man celebrated in the philosophies of white males doesn't reflect "spiritual evolution cuz its empty & godliness // is plenty is ripe & fertile" (45). Shange rejects their denigration of the body and emotions. Her model for perfection is not the Western God's transcendence of the emotional and material worlds, but the African Gods and Goddesses' expression of the life force. But though the lady in blue has made a metaphysical commitment to emotional vulnerability and sexual expression as positive goods, she still does not have a lover.

In the final poem of "no more love poems," the poet confesses her inability to make her experience congruent with her philosophy. Indeed the disparity between her vision and her reality begins to drive her mad: "i've lost it // touch with reality" (45), she confesses. She ponders again the alternatives and admits she does not have the answer: "bein alive & bein a woman & bein colored is a metaphysical //

dilemma i havent conquered yet" (45). She concludes with a reaffirmation of the paradox: "my spirit is too ancient to understand the
separation of // soul & gender / my love is too delicate to have
thrown // back on my face" (45). Though she has not found a solution,
she has achieved clarity about the problem and confidence in her own
values and worth. She will not be likely again to deny her pain or to
take abuse in relationships. She may not be able to find a man to
love her, but she can at least refuse to be a victim, and this is an important step. The other women join her in her refusal to take abuse,
asserting that their love is too "delicate," "beautiful," "sanctified,"
"magic," "saturday nite," "complicated," and "music" to have thrown
back in their faces. Their joint affirmation has more power than an
individual assertion because in celebrating their sisterhood with each
other, each woman hears her value affirmed by the others.

Their resolution not to take abuse is put into practice in the
next poem, the story of a woman who "made too much room" for a
man and apparently considered herself worthless when he left her.
The title line of the poem, "somebody almost walked off wid alla
my stuff" (49), is a metaphor that works on several levels. On the
literal level it may refer to a man who stole some of a woman's things
and attempted to sell them for money. On a sexual level, "stuff" is
a euphemism for a woman's sexuality and refers to the man's failure
to appreciate her giving of her body. And on the psychological level,
the line refers to a man taking advantage of a woman's vulnerability
and need for love. More than a lament, this poem is a celebration
of a woman's self-respect and resolve not to abase herself for a man.
The poem's humor stems from the literal elaboration of the central
metaphor—visualizing a man stuffing himself into a woman's "two
sizes too small . . . tacky skirts" (49) or trying to sell "somethin of
no value on // a open market" (49), and, finally, "throwin my shit
in the sewar" (50). The lady in green enjoys her metaphor so much
that she even begins to imagine this man has taken all her unique
individuality, including her gestures and the identifying marks on her
body. A sense of humor once again transforms pain into self-affirmation: "now give me my stuff / i see ya hidin my laugh / & how i //
sit wif my legs open sometimes / to give my crotch // some sunlight /

& there goes my love my toes . . . my rhythms & my voice . . . this is some delicate // leg & whimsical kiss" (50), she says. In creating a catalogue of her "stuff" she comes to value herself in all her particularity. Instead of being turned in on herself, her anger is directed at the man who didn't appreciate what she had to offer: "i want my own things / how i lived them // & give me my memories . . . you cant have them or do nothin wit them /// stealin my shit from me / dont make it yrs / it makes it stolen" (50). Though rightly angry at the man, her anger is not a plea for him to love her as she thinks she deserves to be loved. Rather it is the anger of a woman who is learning finally to nurture and value herself. "My stuff," she says, "is the anonymous ripped off treasure // of the year" (51). Her list of what she treasures in herself is healing because she affirms her whole self, not just the self that has been primped and pampered to meet male approval. Shange deliberately celebrates aspects of her self that flout cultural ideals of female attractiveness: her immodesty, when she gives her crotch sunlight; her flawed body, including "calloused feet" and a "leg wit the // flea bite"; her unfeminine personality expressed in "quik language" (50); and her unfeminine female smells, when she "didnt get a chance to take a douche" (51).

The lady in blue wonders what the lady will do if this man comes back saying he's sorry. This provokes the women to join together in creating a litany of excuses men give when they say they're sorry, from "'i dont know // how she got yr number baby'" (51) to "'i'm only human, and inadequacy is what makes us human'" (52). The lady in blue replies, "one thing i dont need // is any more apologies" (52). Instead of continuing to live out the forgiving female role, she expresses in yet another particular way the women's joint decision to take no more abuse.

At last able to affirm themselves as they are, colored, and sometimes sorry, open and in need of love, the women face a final challenge as the lady in red tells the story of Crystal and Beau Willie Brown. The story begins in the room of Beau Willie, a Vietnam veteran sent to "kill vietnamese children" (55), who returned "crazy as hell" (55) and addicted to drugs. "There waz no air" (55) in Beau Willie's room where he lay in his sweat, "tucked the sheet // into his limbs like he waz an ol frozen bundle of chicken" (55), drank coffee, wine, water, or took "some blow or some shit / anythin" to make him forget (55). Spotlights reminded him of sieges in Vietnam and he would "get under the // covers & wait for an all clear" (55). Not unaware of the oppressive forces that turned Beau Willie crazy, the lady in red focuses on his interaction with Crystal, age twenty-two, who had "been // his girl since she waz thirteen" (55) and who with their children takes the brunt of Beau Willie's rage.

Before he left for Vietnam, Beau Willie had denied he was the father of Crystal's child, but after he came back he got Crystal pregnant again, and then "most beat // her to death when she tol him" (56). Finally, after hearing that "beau waz spendin alla his money // on the bartendin bitch down at the merry-go-round cafe . . . crystal had gone & // got a court order sayin beau willie brown had no access // to his children" (56). But Beau Willie decided to marry Crystal to claim higher veterans' benefits. The court order, however, didn't stop him from coming over and "beatin crystal with the high chair & her son" until "crystal most died" (57). Later Beau comes back and kicks the door in, screaming how he wants to marry Crystal. Crystal refuses and holds tight to the children to keep them from him, threatening to kill him if he touches them. When Beau Willie "jumped back all humble & apologetic" (58) and his manner softened, Crystal's little girl, Naomi Kenya, ran to him "cryin / daddy, daddy // come back daddy" (59). And "beau willie oozed kindness & // crystal who had known so lil / let beau hold kwame" (59). Among the most painful in the choreopoem, these lines express the Black woman's vulnerability: Crystal allowed Beau to hold her child only because she (like her little daughter) was so starved for love and kindness. But Beau took advantage of her wavering and "jumped up a laughin & a gigglin / a howlin & a hollerin /// awright bitch . . . you gonna marry me" (59). When Crystal refused again he "kicked the screen outta the window / & held the kids offa the sill" still screaming "you gonna marry me" (59) and Crystal said yes, but when Beau Willie told her to scream her acceptance to the neighbors, Crystal "stood by beau in the window / with naomi reachin // for me / & kwame screamin mommy mommy from the fifth // story / but i cd only whisper / & he dropped em" (60). No response seems possible. The ladies on stage are hushed.

The lady in red breaks the silence with her cry, "i waz missin somethin" (60). Her cry reminds everyone of the loss of her children. The other women deepen her cry, adding, "somethin so important," "somethin promised" (60). The lady in blue finally names what is missing—"a layin on of hands," to which the other ladies respond, "strong," "cool," "movin," "makin me whole," "sense," "pure," "all the gods comin into me / layin me open to myself" (61). Their words describe the sensations felt in a laying on of hands, an ancient healing ritual that is often practiced in evangelical sects in poor white and poor Black communities. The ladies explain that a laying on of hands is not sex with a man, or a mother's comforting touch, but a touching in which powers larger than the self are channeled into the one being healed. The laying on of hands ritual affirms the self's position in a community and in the universe, and suggests to her that she is not alone, that other humans—in this case women—and the very powers of being support her life and health. The laying on of hands in a community of women celebrates the power of sisterhood and sharing as one of the keys to a woman's moving through the experience of nothingness.[12]

In the last poem, the lady in red describes how a woman, possibly Crystal, moves through nothingness to new being. Having contemplated suicide, this woman "fell into a numbness" (63), but a mystical experience in nature brought her back to life. As she describes it:

> the only tree i cd see
> took me up in her branches
> held me in the breeze
> made me dawn dew
> that chill at daybreak
> the sun wrapped me up swingin rose light everywhere
> the sky laid over me like a million men
> i waz cold / i waz burnin up / a child
> & endlessly weaving garments for the moon
> wit my tears   (63)

Like Chopin's Edna at the sea, Atwood's protagonist in the woods, and Lessing's Martha walking by the Thames, Shange's lady feels a connection between her rhythms of being and those of nature. Like Shange felt after her experience with the rainbow, the lady in red could conclude, "we are the same as the sky. We are here, breathing, living creatures, and we have a right to everything."[13]

The final words of the lady in red, which are picked up and sung gospel style by the other women, are an incredible affirmation of her own power of being: "i found god in myself // and i loved her / i loved her fiercely" (63). These words express the affirmation of self, of being woman, of being Black, which is at the heart of *for colored girls.* This indeed is the "righteous gospel," the "song of her possibilities" (5), which the lady in brown called for at the beginning of the choreo-poem. These final lines express Shange's conviction that the Black woman's quest for being is grounded in the powers of being. Though she has moments of despair that make her consideration of suicide logical, the powers of being in nature and sisterhood aid the Black woman in moving through nothingness. More than just a statement of self-affirmation, this woman's finding God in herself is an ac-knowledgment of her self's grounding in larger powers.

Shange's statement "i found god in myself" may be shocking to those who usually think of God as a masculine presence. Though most sophisticated Jewish and Christian thinkers would deny that they think of God as an old white man in the sky, the unconscious association of deity with maleness is perpetuated by language and symbol. The African tribal woman has long had her body and skin color affirmed as the image of divinity. But to the Black woman raised with pictures of a blond, blue-eyed Jesus, Shange's affirmation of the God in herself is a revelation of a new way of viewing the world and being a woman. To say "i found god in myself // and i loved her / i loved her fiercely" is to say in the clearest possible terms that it is all right to be a woman, that the Black woman does not have to imitate whiteness or depend on men for her power of being. This affirmation is a clear vision of new being on the far side of nothingness.

# 8. Toward Wholeness: A Vision of Women's Culture

Looking at women's spiritual quest in the works of Kate Chopin, Margaret Atwood, Doris Lessing, Adrienne Rich, and Ntozake Shange has revealed certain similarities. The *experience of nothingness* is central in each. Edna Pontellier finds a life centered on children and conventional marriage empty. The protagonist of *Surfacing* loses her ability to feel when she allows her lover to make the decision about her abortion. Martha Quest's inability to find an image of a creative and free woman leads her into years of drifting. Rich writes of women suppressing their feelings and sensitivities in order to live with men who have learned not to feel as deeply as women do. And Shange's ladies consider suicide in a society where Black women's beauty is unrecognized.

*Mystical awakenings* in nature provide each woman with images of her own power. Edna awakens to her own freedom and value through her union with the great power in the sea. The protagonist of *Surfacing* immerses herself in the transformative powers of life and death in nature and thus grounds her refusal to be a victim. Martha senses her connection to powers while on the veld in Africa, while walking by the Thames, and when she "tunes in" to the currents and forces of energy around her. Rich finds solace in comparing the patterns of her life to the play of the moon's light over ancient Stonehenge and imagines women's creativity as a life force—an underground river, or a weed flowering in tar. Shange's lady feels her being taken up and embraced by a tree and names god in herself.

Not all of the women experience great powers in society or community. Edna does not find the powers of being in a social movement or community, and this may be why she sees no other end to her quest than to return to the one power of being she has known—the sea. Atwood's protagonist does not cement her insight in social or communal mysticism, and thus the ending of *Surfacing* is inconclusive. Martha connects to impersonal currents and forces of energy that she believes are moving toward apocalypse—and, she hopes, also toward rebirth. For Rich and Shange mystical connections with other women, living and dead, who have suffered, nurtured, and struggled, give women strength to create new modes of being for women in the world.

Each woman begins a *new naming* of self and world. Each rejects negative body images and names her body's power anew. Edna exults in the strength of her body after she learns to swim. *Surfacing*'s protagonist gives up her old view of her body as passive and victimized when she learns to see her body as the incarnation of life and death powers. Martha learns to view her body as a sensitive instrument that she can tune to pick up currents of energy. Through her lesbian experiences, Rich comes to a new appreciation of the beauty of women's bodies and sexuality. Shange names the beauty of Black women's bodies and affirms their sensuality.

The drive for wholeness and for the integration of spiritual and social quests is part of the new naming. After her experience in the sea Edna seeks to integrate her newfound spirituality and sensuality; she wants the whole life of a free woman, including sexuality and creativity. *Surfacing*'s protagonist rejects what was *for her* the false freedom associated with her abortion and decides to have a child. This is an attempt to unite her connection to nature with her freedom to make decisions about her body and her life. For Rich, men's separation of reason and feeling, power and sensitivity, is the root of crises in personal and political life. She names women's sensitivity to life and growth as the force that may stem the tide of poverty and violence created by male politics. Shange explicitly rejects the dualism of soul and body, reason and emotion, when she affirms the centrality of emotionality, sexuality, and dance in the Black woman's being.

The patterns of spiritual quest discovered in women's literature have also begun to emerge in other art and ritual forms created by women. The themes expressed in women's literature are part of a new underlying sensibility, a "sacred story," which is surfacing in women's culture as a whole.[1] While it is obviously impossible in this chapter to examine all the new forms created by women, a brief consideration of women's music, women's art, and women's spirituality will reveal the common threads of women's quest.

The lyrics and melodies of feminist songwriters and musicians reflect women's spiritual quest, especially the themes of nothingness, connection to nature, and sisterhood. The experience of nothingness surfaces in several of Meg Christian's songs. In "The Hive," she compares a wedding to a queen bee's approach to the hive of her incarceration and eventual death. In a more personal song, "Scars," Christian sings, "Yes, I'm happy now," but adds that she is often "still caught unawares / By ghosts lurking in my nightmares." The haunting refrain of the song names the experience of nothingness as "ancient loneliness / And ancient pain / And the old scars / And the old scars / Ache again."[2] Cris Williamson alludes to the primal pains and terrors of women in "Wild Things" and urges women to stop holding on to their nightmares. "Go back into the darkness / Like the wild thing that your are," she sings to the fears that haunt her. "Wild, wild things can turn on you," she reminds women, "And you got to set them free."[3] In her powerful "Song of the Soul," which she often encourages audiences to sing with her, Williamson sings of rebirth on the far side of nothingness. "'Love of my life' I am crying, I am not dying, I am dancing," she belts out, as she urges everyone to join with her: "Why don't you sing this song, why don't you sing along / And we can sing for a long, long time."[4] Singing together, Williamson's audiences affirm their new being in a communal ritual.

Women's connections to nature are celebrated in Holly Near's "Water Come Down." In this song Near recalls summer flood irrigation on the farm where she grew up. "Water is like magic, it makes a child feel small," she recalls, "Makes me think that there was something more / Than summer going on for all the . . . Children in the pasture where the waters flow."[5] The "something more than summer" was a sense of connection to the powers of being Holly experienced as a child. In "Waterfall," Cris Williamson sees water as an image for the changing rhythms of hopefulness and despair in a woman's life. Repeating the refrain, "Filling up and spilling over," she reminds women that "when you open up your life to the living, all things come spilling in on you," and "you got to spill some over."[6] In the rhythm of filling up and spilling over, a woman experiences the connection of her emotional life to natural cycles, and she trusts that transformations will occur. Kay Gardner, a flutist, guitarist, and singer whose haunting, primarily musical compositions in her two albums, *Mooncircles* and *Emerging,* are intended to recall ancient women's music, believes that natural rhythms are the essence of music. "The basic form of our inner universe-selves and the outer universe is the circle, or sphere, as Pythagoras and Theana found in theorizing the 'music of the spheres.' The ancients knew this instinctively . . . the moon, the sun, the cycles of life . . . death . . . rebirth . . . seasonal and constant," she writes. Gardner believes that women recognize their connections to cyclic forms because of menstruation and childbirth and that women have a special role to play in restoring cyclical consciousness to all of humankind. Thus she asserts of the circular form she uses in her musical compositions, "Female form in music is the recognition of Nature . . . The music that now assaults our ears and bodies with its vibrations, unhealthy and anti-Nature, is built from the sounds of decaying cities. I believe that our world can change when the vibrations of Nature are respected once more and are duplicated through Women's Music."[7] The circle, which also emerges as a key symbol in women's art, is a powerful image of the impulse toward wholeness in women's culture.

Many of Holly Near's songs celebrate the powers of being that emerge in women's relationships. A form of communal mysticism is strongly affirmed in Near's ecstatic song to her biological sister, "You've Got Me Flying," where she sings, "I'm flying / You inspired a sister song."[8] In "Old Time Woman," Near sings about connections between an old woman rocking on her porch and a young woman with an unexpected pregnancy. "We talked about a lot of things I never thought she would have understood," the young woman sings incredulously, "but that old time woman, she did real good." And in the most powerful line in the song, the old woman affirms her link with the young girl whose life is so different from her own, when she tells her, "If I had not suffered, you wouldn't be wearing those jeans / Being an old time woman, ain't as bad as it seems."[9] In "Fight Back," Near urges women to recognize their common oppression and to join in struggle together. "Every color, religion, and age / One thing we've got in common," she observes ironically, "We can all be battered and raped."[10] In "Sister," Cris Williamson sings of the healing powers that emerge when women share their stories: "I will be the one / To help you ease your pain. / Lean on me, I am your sister / Believe in me, I am your friend."[11] Through compositions that are often wordless, Kay Gardner affirms and creates a sisterhood that unites women of today to their ancient heritage. "I believe that music as a non-verbal means of group meditation can build a unity in women that no political rhetoric can duplicate,"[12] she writes.

Though all the themes of women's quest can be found in every medium, the themes of affirmation of women's bodies and women's connection to nature are prominent in women's art. Like Kay Gardner, Judy Chicago makes the circle a central symbol in her work. In *Through the Flower,* she discusses the emergence of circular forms in her work as a positive affirmation of the female body. "I wanted to express what it was like to be organized around a central core, my vagina, that which made me a woman. I was interested in a dissolving sensation, like one experiences in orgasm."[13] In a series of images created in the mid-1970s, Chicago painted abstract portraits of herself and famous women from history with the circle, the curve, the flower, and the butterfly as primary forms in the compositions. In the painting on the cover of *Through the Flower,* Chicago created a circular soft green form that seems to have an inner source of illumination, surrounded by rounded pink fleshy forms. The center image symbolizes an open receptive vagina and is surrounded by folds of soft pink flesh, a woman's body. The colors in the central core and the surrounding pink forms dissolve into lighter and darker shades, reflecting Chicago's discovery that she could represent "receptiveness through softer swirling color, the state of orgasm through color that dissolved."[14]

Chicago's massive art piece, "The Dinner Party," which was

displayed in the San Francisco Museum of Modern Art in the spring and early summer of 1979, featured a large triangular table set for thirty-nine famous women of mythology and history. The first place was for the primordial Goddess and the last for artist Georgia O'Keeffe. An evocation of sisterhood and herstory, Chicago's piece was also a celebration of the female body, for each plate was shaped and painted to represent an abstract image of the vagina and the triangular shape of the table echoed the pubic triangle celebrated in ancient sculptures of Goddesses.[15] Some people have wondered about Chicago's near obsession with imagery derived from the female body. In *Through the Flower,* Chicago explains it: "On the one hand, it was through my cunt that I made contact with Lloyd, who affirmed me and gave me great pleasure, especially at the moment of orgasm, when I was totally vulnerable and exposed and loved for being in that state. At the same time, because I had a cunt, I was despised by society. By making an image of the sensation of orgasm, I was trying to affirm the fact of being female and thus implicitly challenge male superiority."[16] All of Chicago's recent art provides women with images that affirm their female bodies.

Like Chicago, Mary Beth Edelson also celebrates the female body in her art. The image of the circle frequently appears in her work as well. Edelson even sees the circle as representing her process of creation: "I see my process as being circular/spiraling/encompassing. Circular because I go over the same ground of concerns, and spiraling on different levels, hoping to gain more insight on each passing."[17] In a series of four photographs of herself, naked, with the images retouched with radiating, swirling, white and black lines, representing energy forces and centers, Edelson celebrates the female body and its connections to nature. Of this series Edelson wrote, "I am depicting the wholistic, centered, assertive, sexual, spiritual woman who is in the process of becoming, balancing her mind/body/spirit. I am using my body in these rituals as a stand-in for the Goddess, as a stand-in for Every woman."[18] The small breasts, generously curved thighs, pubic hair, and signs of age in Edelson's own body are an effective testimony to the creative potential of all women's bodies. In another series, Edelson records her pilgrimage to a cave in Yugoslavia, said to be the site of Neolithic Goddess worship.[19] In much of Edelson's work, the boundary between art and ritual is blurred. Her solitary pieces were created to connect both the artist and observer to the contemplative or meditative center within themselves. Some of Edelson's other works are performance pieces, which, in requiring the participation of a group of women, create a community and thus embody the principle of sisterhood.

Feminist art critic Lucy Lippard has noted the prominence of imagery of the body and nature and noted the connections between women's art and ritual. Lippard's theories about women's art are rooted in her own experience. As she says, "nature—contact with the land and the sea—is what keeps me alive and more or less sane . . . because I am a woman, because the hills and waves echo my own sense of my body, its potential for growth, its rhythms and round- ness. I see that same pleasure in identification with the sensuous forms and skins of the earth expressed in much art by women that depicts or emerges from or is built in nature."[20] Lippard finds the recurrence of a "central ovoid motif, often perceptible as an enclosure or aperture," echoing the forms of nature, and foreshadowing Chicago's more ex- plicit vaginal forms, typical of the work of Georgia O'Keeffe and Emily Carr. In the work of Mexican artist Frieda Kahlo, "there is a sense of longing for connection with an anthropomorphized earth mother," which was represented, for example, in a 1943 work called *Roots* where "the artist reclines, fully clothed, on a barren rocky plain with a great, many-stemmed plant growing through a cavity in her chest."[21] Lippard discovered similar patterns of symbolism relating women's bodies and nature in the work of many other women artists, including Carolee Schneemann, Anna Mendieta, Ricki Blau, Jody Pinto, Ulrike Rosenbach, and Chicago. She also found that when women artists like Margaret Hicks, Alice Aycock, Colette, Nil Yalter, and Ree Marton created earthwork sculptures—monumental outdoor pieces using earth and natural materials—they, more often than men, created a link to the monumental piece by enacting a ritual around or in it. According to Lippard the significance of the ritual is to create a connection between the artist and nature.

Gloria Feman Orenstein corroborates Lippard's conclusions

about the prominence of imagery of the body and nature, and the close connection of art and ritual in the work of contemporary women artists. The works she considers evoke a form of consciousness in which "divinity was seen to reside in matter and the energies of the earth were revered as sacred."[22] In the works of many artists, Orenstein finds that women's identification with nature is expressed through symbolism associated with ancient Goddess worship.

In the grassroots women's spirituality movement, the same themes of mysticism, celebration of women's bodies and their connections to nature and each other, and the drive for wholeness are also apparent. *WomanSpirit* magazine,[23] first published in 1974, is a place where women in the United States share spiritual experiences and insights. Many of the articles in *WomanSpirit* celebrate women's connection to nature. Jean Mountaingrove's "Explorations in the Grove," printed in *WomanSpirit*'s first issue, is eloquent and also typical. Describing herself standing in a "small tree-circled space in a natural wilderness," Mountaingrove writes, "Here I feel nurtured, grateful. Time stands still. Eternity is present ... The pools of water here are quiet, unmoving—only a few inches deep—yet as I look into them I feel the clear flow of life which wells up in me continuously—my life flow which is *the* life flow, reflected for a moment as eternity."[24] Like some other women in the spirituality movement, Mountaingrove named herself after the place where she experienced great power.

In *WomanSpirit* many women have written about how a new sense of their connection to nature has changed their feelings about their bodies. Chellis Glendinning thought about coordinating her menstrual cycles with the moon's cycles for months, and when it happened on her twenty-eighth birthday, she wrote, "I felt myself retreating into my depths. I left a dinner party to be alone. As I walked around among the trees in darkness I began to feel a heavy sadness in my belly like the dong of a deep mourning bell. I began to cry, and I felt myself letting go—of the food-blood inside me, of a child never born, of my dear cat who had died, of a relationship which had grown stale ... The blood began to flow just then, and it was redder and brighter than before. That night I slept sound and content."[25]

Though the experiences that initially inspired *WomanSpirit* usually happened in solitude, after sharing their stories and hearing their experiences confirmed, many women have begun to come to-gether in groups of two or three or more to celebrate their shared spirituality. In the summer of 1975 *WomanSpirit* held a five-day festival during which 200 women lived on the land and shared dreams, knowledge, skills.[26] According to one of the participants, Hallie Mountain Wing (Iglehart), "In the openness, support and love that we created, we were able to be who we really are: full, free women." For Hallie Iglehart the experience was more than a five-day respite from ordinary life. "There was such an exchange of appreciation (how long have we been unappreciated?) that I know I'll never feel the insecurity and need for feedback that I used to feel."[27]

Ritual forms are spontaneously emerging in every area of women's culture, not just from those whose special interest is spiri-tuality. As was discussed in chapter one, consciousness raising can be seen as a ritual in which stories are shared and sisterhood is affirmed, and women's fiction and poetry readings can be seen as rituals where women gather to hear their experiences and visions named. In Shange's work, poetry readings literally spilled over into dance and ritual forms. Women's music can inspire a meditative frame of mind, and when the audience joins with the singer, women's concerts also are transformed into ritual affirmations of women's shared experience and visions of new being. An impulse toward ritual affirmation of women's connec-tions to nature and each other has also emerged in women's art. The blurring of the boundaries between ritual and literature, music, and art is yet another expression of the movement toward wholeness in women's culture and is also to return ritual, art, music, and literature to the unity they have in less-differentiated cultures.

In the new rituals, the underlying story and new visions of power in women's spiritual quest are named, shared, and publicly acknowledged. As Kay Turner has noted, "the participation in ritual by men has been their most profound display of cultural authority and their most direct access to it."[28] Because women have been ex-cluded from publicly acknowledged power, for women to "create rituals which emphasize their loyalty to each other and finally name the powers which men have found 'anomalous' (i.e., nameless) is indeed an ultimate, radical (proceeding from the root) affirmation of the revolutionary potential of the feminist movement."[29] Women's rituals simultaneously name, validate, and create new possibilities of being for women in a new world—new culture and new community. Participating in a ritual of the new naming brings women's experiences and visions out into the open and through sharing transforms them from private into public reality. Through ritual women gain confidence to act on their feelings and values. Turner is correct when she says that "what is stressed through ritual is the dynamic quality of power, the continuous exchange of gifts which heightens the identity of all who participate."[30] Moreover, it seems to be characteristic of women's rituals that hierarchicalism is minimized. In sharing their visions, most writers, artists, singers, and ritualists acknowledge that their works have emerged out of experiences that are shared by other women and are namings of insights that other women will recognize because their experiences are similar.

Women's rituals affirm the sisterhood and power of women. Many also affirm the grounding of women's power in nature. Some women also have begun to name the power that is celebrated in women's rituals "Goddess." To name God in oneself, or to speak the word "Goddess" again after many centuries of silence is to reverse age-old patterns of thinking in which male power and female subordination are viewed as the norm. When Barbry My Own and Hallie Mountain Wing used the word "Goddess" in a ritual Barbry explained what they meant by the word: "We have not defined 'Goddess' except in the loose terms, 'womanenergy.' We hope to invoke a materialization of that woman energy, to love it, play with it, to exult in it."[31] The power which Barbry My Own describes is within and without. Though Goddess has yet to become a familiar name, the word is being spoken more and more often. And many women feel chills of recognition as they hear the word, which names the legitimacy and beneficence of female power.[32] The reemergence of the Goddess in contemporary culture gathers together many of the themes of women's spiritual quest. It is a new naming of women's power, women's bodies, women's feelings of connection to nature, and women's bonds with each other.

From this brief consideration of women's music, women's art, women's rituals, and women's spirituality, it is clear that the themes of women's spiritual quest in women's literature are but one reflection of an underlying sacred story, a new understanding of self and a new orientation in the world, which is emerging in a variety of cultural forms as women give voice to their experience. A drive toward wholeness, toward healing the splits between people and nature, body and soul, reason and emotion, culture and experience, is evident in all the forms in which women's spiritual quest is expressed.

The new naming of women's bodies and connections to nature that emerges as part of the drive toward wholeness in women's spiritual quest has provoked controversy even within circles of women thinkers. Some feel that the association between women and nature is a legacy of the oppressive stereotyped thinking that has limited women's role to bearing and rearing children. Some believe that in naming women's bodies and nature anew insufficient attention is paid to the specifically human values of freedom from or control over the body, nature, and irrationality. For example, Judith Plaskow expressed her fear that in "neglecting the human dimension of responsibility to nature ... we may think of ourselves as more determined by nature than we really are."[33] Others feel that celebration of women's connections to the body and nature is at best a harmless diversion and at worst draws attention away from the realities of dominance and oppression, justice and injustice, which inspire feminist (and other) political struggles.

I would argue that rather than ignoring or denying feelings of connection to nature, women (and others) need to develop a new understanding of being human, in which the body is given a more equal footing with the intellect and the human connection to nature is positively valued at the same time that the awesome (but not un-limited) human capacity to manipulate and control nature is recognized. This view will not be a new monism in which differences between the body and mind or nature and freedom are denied, but it will be a more integrated view in which the differences are not viewed in hierarchical and oppositional ways. In proposing that a new theory of human nature be developed, I agree with Lucy Lippard that women's intermediary position between nature and culture is "seen as a disad-vantage only because of overwhelming conditioning in favor of male-dominated, anti-natural culture."[34] In the present cultural situation where recognition of the human grounding in nature is a crucial cultural imperative, women's supposed disadvantage becomes an advantage: women are in a good position to begin to develop new, less dualistic understandings of the human relation to nature and freedom. As Lucy Lippard has said, "Most female culture in fact *includes* nature and natural processes, while recognizing a continuity with other than human forms."[35] Women's culture expresses a vision of a more integrated view of the relation between nature and freedom. It remains for feminist philosophers, thealogians,[36] and others to weave the threads of women's visions into a new theory of human nature. This process has begun, but like all efforts at cultural transformation it will take a long time.

Though the danger of simply reversing the old dualisms will remain as long as women simply react (and those in power force them to react) against their historic subordination and its rooting in the classic dualisms, I like to think that women's celebration of the body, nature, feeling, and intuition as the first stage in an attempt—which surely cannot be fully successful on the first try—to move toward a more whole way of thinking. I like to think that in this new mode of thinking, the body, nature, emotion, and intuition will be affirmed, but also reason, freedom, and the spirit will not be left behind. I like to think about spiritual insights arising from connection to the body and nature, to imagine forms of understanding in which the body plays a part, and to begin to conceptualize a view of human freedom in which limitation by nature, death, and finitude is accepted.

The drive to integrate the spiritual and the social quests also arises out of the impulse toward wholeness in women's quest. Dualistic thinking encourages a separation of the spiritual from the social, but whole thinking looks forward to the realization of spiritual insight in social reality. Since women's spiritual experience leads to a new sense of their own powers of being, women will not likely consider the contemplative life, which some religions have glorified, as the most appropriate expression of their new insight. In a supportive community, women will be eager to point out the false naming of power and value within patriarchy and to begin to name self, power, and value anew based on their experiences. They will be eager to create new ways of being for women in a new social world.

The connections between women's spiritual quest and women's social quest have been intuitively recognized by many women whose spiritual experiences have provided them with energy and vision to make changes in their lives and to work to change women's position in culture and society. Recently women have begun to write about the connections between spirituality and personal and social change.[37] They have pointed out that women's spiritual quest provides new visions of individual and shared power that can inspire a transformation of culture and society. New understandings of power as arising from connection to the body and nature, and as shared grounding in the powers of being that emerge in nature and community, can be used to challenge the assumption of patriarchal culture that power comes from control and domination of nature and other people. Women's rituals create a space in which women's visions of power can be experienced and healing of ancient pains can occur. By enabling women to recognize the grounding of their lives in the ground of being, women's spiritual quest gives women the strength to create alternatives to personal relationships and social institutions where women's value is not recognized. Women's spiritual quest thus is not an alternative to women's social quest, but rather is one dimension of the larger quest women have embarked upon to create a new world.

# Afterword to the Third Edition

Women's stories have not been told. And without stories there is no articulation of experience. Without stories a woman is lost when she comes to make the important decisions of her life. She does not learn to value her struggles, to celebrate her strengths, to comprehend her pain. Without stories she is alienated from those deeper experiences of self and world that have been called spiritual or religious. She is closed in silence. The expression of women's spiritual quest is integrally related to the telling of women's stories. If women's stories are not told, the depth of women's souls will not be known.

THE COINCIDENCE that I was asked to write an afterword for a fifteenth anniversary edition of *Diving Deep and Surfacing* when *Odyssey with the Goddess*[1] was in press, provided me with the opportunity to reflect on the connections between the two books. In the first, I analyze spiritual quest in the work of women writers; in the second, I am the writer, telling the story of my own spiritual quest. When I wrote that women's stories *must* be told, I never imagined that one day *I* would feel compelled to tell my own story or remain "closed in silence," "alienated from those deeper experiences of self and world that have been called spiritual or religious."

When I wrote that women's stories must be told, I was naming the life-giving power I felt when I found elements of my experience articulated in stories written by other women. I was a young white woman educated at the best universities, yet traumatized and silenced by patriarchal values and authority. Mine had seemingly been an ordinary middle-class childhood in the tract home suburbs that sprung up in Los Angeles after the Second World War. But if my childhood was ordinary for a woman of my age and class, then trauma was the ordinary experience of girls. Part of that trauma was being closed in silence.

The command to "control yourself," which was repeated throughout my childhood and followed by punishment if I did not comply, convinced me that I had no right to my feelings, whether positive or negative. Children were to be seen and not heard. A girl was expected to do what she was told and play quietly by herself. My father spent endless hours training my brothers to play baseball. My mother and I watched. Very little attention was given to me. I was a good child. I didn't seem to need anything. I was also a shy and withdrawn child, unable to express the feelings I had been taught to control. No one seemed to notice. No one encouraged me to tell the stories that were bottled up inside.

In school I got A's by doing what I was told to do. When I, who had gone to a high school where most of the other kids got married in their teens, received a scholarship to attend a major university, I considered myself lucky. For me the university was a completely unknown world. I had no familiarity with anything I was asked to study. I did not know who Plato was or whether he came before or after Hobbes and Locke. But I learned how to study and soon was making A's, while becoming initiated into the world of values and assumptions created by the "great thinkers of the Western world." It never crossed my mind to ask why none of them were women.

When I received a scholarship to attend a prestigious graduate school, I thought I had finally won the right to state my own tentative opinions about the great male thinkers whose ideas, I still believed, expressed the highest truth. But whenever I tried, I was given to understand that my point of view was not worthy of consideration. Conversations with professors often ended with my breaking into uncontrollable tears. And it was clear that my tears, like my words, were unacceptable.

I was well-educated, but when it came to expressing all that was closed inside me, it was as if I had never been taught to speak, let alone write. I often felt that no one understood me. My inability

to speak, and when I spoke, to be heard, brought me close to a
breakdown. Either I was crazy or something was terribly wrong with
the world around me.

Sometimes my sense of isolation seemed so overpowering that
I, like Ntozake Shange's women, considered suicide. I know that I
might not have survived my twenties if I had not found aspects of
my experience articulated in the words of the women I wrote about
in *Diving Deep and Surfacing.* Nor my thirties without the increas-
ing chorus of women's voices that began to emerge in the wake of
the women's movement. Women's stories provided insight, wisdom,
and strength, but they did not heal the persistent despair I felt.

The "Preface to the Second Edition" of this book described a
turning point in my journey as a writer and a teacher, and in my spiritual quest. I had gone to lecture in Amsterdam thinking of myself as
an academic, albeit one who integrated experience and scholarship
in her teaching and writing. I knew that if I wanted to have an academic job, scholarship had to be given priority over experience in my
work. It was not always an easy balance to maintain, yet it seemed
like a fair and reasonable expectation.

But in Amsterdam, the women theological students who heard
me speak told me that my work provoked them to devote consider-
able classroom time to the telling of their own stories. Of course the
stories of my students had been evoked by the works we studied and
had exploded and erupted into my classes. But I had never considered giving my students' stories — or my own — the kind of time
and space that the Dutch women had given to theirs. Why not?
Because it would not have been considered "academic." I had been
taught to maintain a strict boundary between teaching and what was
contemptuously called — even by other women academics — mere
"consciousness raising." If consciousness was raised in the course of
my teaching, fine, but the focus of the classroom had to remain on
works written by others.

When I left Amsterdam and went on to teach in an experimen-
tal women's studies program in Lesbos, I allowed my priorities to
shift. Writing and telling our own stories became as important as the
material we read. When our own experiences became central, so did

our pain. Almost all of us had been traumatized. And all of us were closed in silence. In the sharing of our stories, we began to heal the deep wounds that had festered because our stories *could not* be told.

Sharing stories with other women in a classroom setting gave me the courage to write in the first person in the "Preface to the Second Edition" and to begin to incorporate aspects of my experience in much of my subsequent writing, for example, in *Laughter of Aphrodite*.[2]

But experience was not easily integrated into an academic setting. In Lesbos, I was not only a teacher, but like my students, a woman emerging from silence, through pain, to healing of body, mind, and soul. Yet, students still had to turn in an analytical paper if they wanted a grade, and I had to judge their work by standards other than those that had emerged in our work together. It is not surprising that few of the women who were taking the Lesbos courses for credit ever completed the written work. Nor that my experiences in Lesbos made it more difficult to step back into the role of authority (lectures) and authoritarianism (grading) that was expected of me in my teaching job at San Jose State.

In addition, it was not easy to incorporate the personal voice that was emerging in my work with the more distanced voice of an academic. The more I told my own story, the farther I moved from acceptable subject matters and acceptable modes of discourse. I thought I had done a brilliant job of combining passion and analysis in a lecture I gave at Harvard Divinity School.[3] At a meeting of women faculty called to discuss my lecture, a senior woman praised the way I integrated scholarship and deep feeling in my presentation. But when she concluded that "we" could never "do" anything like that at Harvard and "be taken seriously," she cut off further discussion of my ideas as effectively as any of my graduate school professors had ever done. Though my lecture had received stunning applause from a standing-room-only crowd, it could not even be discussed among academic women! I began to understand that in telling my story, I was writing myself out of the university.

I had come to the place where I, like Chopin's Edna, felt I had to shed my clothes and swim out to sea. My husband had left me a year previously, so I was free to create my own life. I resigned a tenured full professorship and moved to Lesbos, choosing the embrace of the grey-blue sea over the confining structures of academia. Many of my friends marvelled that I had made such a "brave" decision. It was a brave decision, but it was one I felt compelled to make. I could no longer hold together the contradictions between my commitment to women and our stories, and the demands of the university. And even though I knew how Edna's story ended, I imagined that I could swim naked and alone to freedom.

It was not so simple.

After about a year's time, I came face to face again with the nothingness I had written about in this book. Without structures of work or family to hold me together, to force me to keep going, I was more vulnerable than I had ever been. The dreams I had brought with me to Lesbos had not materialized. Freedom was nowhere in sight. All I could feel was an overpowering loneliness that made all my achievements seem empty. I had expected my writing to sustain me. But I stopped writing when I could not find words that would heal my despair.

In retrospect, I can see that, painful as its consequences were, I made the right decision. If I had stayed in academia, I would have kept functioning, writing, and teaching. I might never have been forced to confront my despair.

My depression persisted for several years. I found strategies to fill in my days, and devoted most of my energy to the struggle to keep thoughts of suicide out of my mind at night. During that time, my mother was diagnosed with cancer. Her dying and death shook me to the core and began a process of healing from what I now see as nearly lifelong despair.

Shortly after my mother died, a friend came to me and said: "Not now but in several months . . . I will ask you to write the story of your mother's dying in relation to the myth of the Mother and Daughter Goddesses. You will sit down and write the essay in a couple of days."[4] On a practical level, my friend was asking me to write a chapter for a book on Demeter and Persephone that she was editing. But on a spiritual level, she was calling me out of the silence that had closed in around me. I heard her words as a command to tell my story. I understood that the telling of my story was the only way out of my isolation, the only way to begin to unravel my despair.

Telling the story of my mother's dying was a beginning, but it was not an ending. In my mother's dying I glimpsed a great love that surrounds us all. I wrote that I believed this was the great mystery revealed at Eleusis. But even this thealogical insight did not lift my despair for long. My thealogy was not firmly rooted in my life. In order for it to become so, I had to go back to the place where my despair began. I had to see what made me believe I was fundamentally alone. I had to go back and tell my story again. I had to tell it over and over until I could see that the truths that emerged in the telling of my story were not congruent with my belief that I was alone in the universe.[5]

As I continued to write the story that began with my mother's dying, I finally gained insight into my despair. I realized that its source was the command to "control yourself." That command meant: your feelings are not valid. No one wants to hear your story. Shroud yourself in silence. Die! As I told my story again and again, I finally understood: my feelings are valid. My story must be told. I am alive.

The story of my healing is told more fully in *Odyssey with the Goddess*. After I finished writing it, one of my oldest and dearest friends commented that while she found my story personally moving, she wondered why I bothered to tell it, since she did not believe it contributed to feminist theology. One answer to her question is simply that I wrote the book because I had to: it was my only way out of a silence that was killing me. Another answer is that it fulfills the intuition I had when I wrote this book. For me the most meaningful mode of writing feminist thealogy is to tell our stories in such a way that we confront the sources of our despair and name anew the great powers that give shape and meaning to our lives.

A growing number of writers in feminist spirituality are telling stories. Christine Downing incorporates her own stories into her work on the Goddess and archetypes of the sacred. Karen McCarthy Brown wove her story into her telling of the story of Mama Lola.

Starhawk is writing novels. Mary Daly, an intellectual autobiography. Women have been enchanted by Clarissa Pinkola Estes's stories of running with wolves.[6]

I believe that this is an important trend. Women are hungry for stories that name our experiences and provide us with models of the possible.[7] But I believe there is a deeper reason for the turn to stories in feminist work in religion. Many of us are telling stories because there is no other way for us to express the new visions of the sacred that emerge as we heal the trauma of having been closed in silence for so long.

*Athens, February 2, 1995*

# Notes

## PREFACE TO THE SECOND EDITION

1. Lynn Andrews, *The Flight of the Seventh Moon* (New York: Harper & Row, 1984), pp. 46–48.

2. Adrienne Rich, "Transcendental Etude," *The Dream of a Common Language* (New York: Norton, 1978), p. 75.

3. See my article "Toward a Paradigm Shift in the Academy and Religious Studies," in Christie Farnham, ed., *Transforming the Consciousness of the Academy* (Bloomington: Indiana University Press, 1986).

4. *Journal of the American Academy of Religion* 44, 2 (1976), pp. 317–25.

5. See *Diving Deep,* pp. 20–22.

6. In an unpublished article, "Wholistic Feminist Philosophy," presented at the 1985 meetings of the National Women's Studies Association.

7. The locus classicus for this view is the vision of the Good in Plato's *Symposium;* see *The Collected Dialogues of Plato in-*

*cluding the Letters,* Edith Hamilton and Huntington Cairns, eds. (New York: Bollingen Series LXXI, Pantheon Books, 1966), p. 562.

8. See "Finitude, Death, and Reverence for Life," forthcoming in *Semeia* and in my next book, *Journey to the Goddess,* and "Toward a Paradigm Shift in the Academy and Religious Studies," in Christie Farnham, ed., *Transforming the Consciousness of the Academy* (Bloomington: Indiana University Press, 1986).

9. Margaret Atwood, *Surfacing* (New York: Simon & Schuster, 1972), p. 182.

10. For information about the International Women's Studies Institute, please write Box 601, San Francisco, California 94133.

11. Christine Downing, *The Goddess* (New York: Crossroad Publishing Company, 1984).

12. Adrienne Rich, *The Dream of a Common Language* (New York: Norton, 1978).

13. *The Homeric Hymns,* Thelma Sargent, trans. (New York: Norton, 1973).

14. Charlene Spretnak, *Lost Goddesses of Early Greece* (Boston: Beacon Press, 1984).

15. Carol P. Christ and Judith Plaskow, eds., *Womanspirit Rising* (New York: Harper & Row, 1979).

16. Nelle Morton, *The Journey Is Home* (Boston: Beacon Press, 1985), p. 55.

17. Adrienne Rich, "Transcendental Etude," in *The Dream of a Common Language* (New York: Norton, 1978), p. 75.

18. Christine Downing, "Persephone in Hades," in *The Goddess* (New York: Crossroad Publishing Company, 1983).

19. Kate Chopin, *The Awakening* (New York: Capricorn Books, 1964), pp. 34, 71, 188.

20. See my "Rituals with Aphrodite," *Anima* 12, 1, pp. 25–33.

21. Margaret Atwood, *Surfacing* (New York: Simon & Schuster, 1972), pp. 196, 197, 206, 210.

22. Adrienne Rich, "Transcendental Etude," *The Dream of a Common Language* (New York: Norton, 1978), p. 74.

## CHAPTER 1.  WOMEN'S STORIES, WOMEN'S QUEST

1. Doris Lessing, *A Proper Marriage* (New York: New American Library, 1970), p. 206.
2. See Judith Plaskow, *Sex, Sin, and Grace: Women's Experience and the Theologies of Reinhold Niebuhr and Paul Tillich* (Washington, D.C.: University Press of America, 1979), pp. 33-47.
3. Stephen Crites, "The Narrative Quality of Experience," *Journal of the American Academy of Religion* 39, 3 (September 1971), p. 295. I have changed the pronoun in Crites's statement. Crites uses the masculine "generic" pronoun because the sense of self and world in most stories is created from a male perspective.
4. Michael Novak, *Ascent of the Mountain, Flight of the Dove: An Invitation to Religious Studies* (New York: Harper & Row, 1971), p. 52.

5.  Crites, p. 295.

6.  For a consideration of why women haven't written their stories, see Tillie Olsen, *Silences* (New York: Delta/Seymour Lawrence, 1979).

7.  Virginia Woolf, *A Room of One's Own* (New York: Harcourt Brace Jovanovich, 1957), p. 86.

8.  Jill Johnston, "The Mothers," *The Village Voice*, October 11, 1973, p. 11.

9.  Nelle Morton, unpublished sermon, "Hearing to Speech," delivered at Claremont School of Theology, Claremont, California, April 27, 1977, p. 1. Also see "The Rising Woman Consciousness in a Male Language Structure," *Andover/Newton Quarterly* 12, 4 (1972), pp. 163–176.

10.  Adrienne Rich, *The Dream of a Common Language* (New York: Norton, 1978), p. 76.

11.  Those feminists who have become critics of women's stories recognize a connection between literature and life and have thus rejected the philosophical commitment of the New Criticism school to the autonomy of the literary text. Fraya Katz-Stoker stated the feminist case against New Criticism clearly when she said, "Feminist criticism can never be merely formal because women recognize out of their own oppression [that] . . . literature is a major component of the educational process that shapes our destiny" (Fraya Katz-Stoker, "The Other Criticism: Feminism vs. Formalism," in Susan Koppelman Cornillon, ed., *Images of Women in Fiction: Feminist Perspectives,* Bowling Green, Ohio: Bowling Green University Popular Press, 1973, p. 326). And Annis Pratt asserted that while the tools of *"textual analysis"* developed by New Criticism could be useful to feminist critics, *"contextual analysis* which considers the relevance of a group of works . . . as a reflection of the situation of women" must complement it (Annis Pratt, "The New Feminist Criticism," *College English,* May 1971, p. 873).

For further consideration of this issue, see Carol P. Christ, "Feminist Studies in Religion and Literature: A Methodological Reflection," *Journal of the American Academy of Religion* 44, 2

(1976), pp. 317–25; Florence Howe, "Feminism and Literature," in Cornillon, ed., *Images of Women in Fiction: Feminist Perspectives,* p. 259; Carolyn Heilbrun, *Toward a Recognition of Androgyny* (New York: Alfred A. Knopf, 1973, p. x; Ellen Moers, *Literary Women: The Great Writers* (New York: Doubleday, 1976), p. xiii; and Elaine Showalter, *A Literature of Their Own: British Women Novelists from Brontë to Lessing* (Princeton: Princeton University Press, 1977), p. 11, all of whom assert literature's relation to life.

12.  See, for example, Robin Morgan, *Going Too Far: The Personal Chronicle of a Feminist* (New York: Random House, 1978).

13.  For a consideration of how this approach to women's spiritual quest compares to other theories of the relation of religion and literature, see Christ, "Feminist Studies in Religion and Literature." Also see David H. Helsa, "Religion and Literature: The Second Stage," *Journal of the American Academy of Religion* 46, 2, pp. 181–192, for a history of religion and literature studies in the U.S. and a survey of recent developments.

14.  Joseph Campbell, *The Hero with a Thousand Faces* (Princeton: Princeton University Press, 1972), pp. 49–243.

15.  Pratt, "The New Feminist Criticism," p. 887.

16.  Crites, p. 295.

17.  See Paul Tillich, *The Courage to Be* (New Haven: Yale University Press, 1968), p. 156.

18.  The above description of the powers of being which are revealed in women's quest is drawn from my analysis of the works to be discussed in the succeeding chapters. It should be noted that the authors of the works to be discussed depict these powers but do not analyze them, and that this is a description of a view of reality which emerges through women's spiritual quest, not a philosophical justification of it.

19.  See for example, Mary Daly, *Beyond God the Father: Toward a Philosophy of Women's Liberation* (Boston: Beacon Press, 1973), esp. pp. 29–43.

20. Naomi Goldenberg, *Changing of the Gods: Feminism and the End of Traditional Religions* (Boston: Beacon Press, 1979), p. 120.

21. I like to think that Margaret Atwood's comments to Dan Noel in a letter dated December 14, 1974, would express the reaction of other women writers to interpretations of spiritual quest in their work. "I didn't set out to create a female religious experience," Atwood said, ". . . though I found Ms. Christ very persuasive (gosh, did I really do all that?)."

## CHAPTER 2. NOTHINGNESS, AWAKENING, INSIGHT, NEW NAMING

1. What follows is a phenomenological description of *a* common pattern in women's spiritual quest, derived from literary analysis and reflection on the relation of experiences depicted in literature to life.

2. For a similar notion, see Sheila Collins, *A Different Heaven and Earth* (Valley Forge: Judson Press, 1974), p. 144.

3. Michael Novak, *The Experience of Nothingness* (New York: Harper & Row, 1970), p. ix.

4. Novak, pp. 115, 15.

5. Mary Daly, "Critics' Choices," *Commonweal* 93, 21 (February 26, 1971), p. 526.

6. Novak, p. 15.

7. Judy Chicago, *Through the Flower: My Struggle as a Woman Artist* (Garden City, N.Y.: Doubleday, 1975), p. 55.

8. See Valerie Saiving, "The Human Situation: A Feminine View," in Carol P. Christ and Judith Plaskow, eds., *Womanspirit Rising* (San Francisco: Harper & Row, 1979), p. 26, and Judith Plaskow, *Sex, Sin, and Grace: Women's Experience and the Theologies of Reinhold Niebuhr and Paul Tillich* (Washington, D.C.: University Press of America, 1979).

9.  See Erich Neumann, "The Psychological Stages of Feminine Development," *Spring* (New York: Analytical Psychology Club of New York, 1959); Nancy Chodorow, "Family Structure and Feminine Personality," in Michelle Zimbalist Rosaldo and Louise Lamphere, eds., *Woman, Culture, and Society* (Stanford: Stanford University Press, 1974), pp. 43–67; and *The Reproduction of Mothering: Psychoanalysis and the Sociology of Gender* (Berkeley: University of California Press, 1978); and Dorothy Dinnerstein, *The Mermaid and the Minotaur* (New York: Harper & Row, 1976).

10. Dorothy Dinnerstein, *The Mermaid and the Minotaur,* pp. 33–34, was the first to suggest that this theory applies to children who are cared for primarily by the mother or another female. If infant care were shared by both male and female parent figures, then both girls and boys would develop similar personalities.

11. William James, *The Varieties of Religious Experience: A Study in Human Nature* (New York: Collier Books, 1961), pp. 299–301.

12. George Harrison, "Within You Without You," from *Sergeant Pepper's Lonely Hearts Club Band* (Capitol Records, Inc., 1967).

13. R. C. Zaehner, *Mysticism: Sacred and Profane* (London: Oxford University Press, 1957), pp. 198-99.

14. Evelyn Underhill, *Mysticism* (New York: Dutton, 1961), p. 81.

15. Freud called attention to the feelings of "limitlessness and of a bond with the universe," which he called the "oceanic feeling," but he considered it a regression to an infantile way of perceiving the world. See Sigmund Freud, *Civilization and Its Discontents,* in The Standard Edition of the *Complete Works,* James Strachey, ed. London: Hogarth Press, 1971), Vol. 21, p. 71.

16. Simone de Beauvoir, *The Second Sex,* H. M. Parshley, trans. and ed. (New York: Bantam Books, 1970), p. 341.

17. See Sherry Ortner, "Is Female to Male as Nature is to Culture?" in *Woman, Culture, and Society,* Michelle Zimbalist Rosaldo and Louise Lamphere, eds. (Stanford: Stanford University Press, 1974), pp. 67-87.

18. Susan Griffin, *Woman and Nature: The Roaring Inside Her* (New York: Harper & Row, 1978), p. 219.
19. Annis Pratt, "Women and Nature in Modern Fiction," *Contemporary Literature* 13, 4 (Fall 1972), p. 488.
20. Mary Daly, *Beyond God the Father* (Boston: Beacon Press, 1974), p. 47.
21. Muriel Rukeyser, "Käthe Kollwitz" (New York: Pocket Books, 1973), p. 73.
22. De Beauvoir, *The Second Sex,* especially pp. xiii–xxix, 456–97. Also see Carol P. Christ, "Motherhood: Spirit and Flesh" (a review of *Of Woman Born*), *Crosscurrents* 28, 2 (Summer 1978), pp. 244–47.
23. See "Motherearth and the Megamachine," in *Womanspirit Rising,* Carol P. Christ and Judith Plaskow, eds. (New York: Harper & Row, 1979), pp. 43–52, and Rosemary R. Ruether, *New Woman/ New Earth: Sexist Ideologies and Human Liberation* (New York: Seabury Press, 1975).

## CHAPTER 3.   SPIRITUAL LIBERATION, SOCIAL DEFEAT: KATE CHOPIN

1. See Margaret Culley, ed., *The Awakening: An Authoritative Text, Context, Criticisms* (New York: Norton, 1976), pp. 146–55, for a selection of "Contemporary Review."
2. Page numbers refer to quotes from the Capricorn Books, 1964 edition of *The Awakening,* introduction by Kenneth Eble.
3. Adrienne Rich, *The Dream of a Common Language* (New York: Norton, 1978), p. 62.
4. Rich, p. 63.
5. Donald A. Ringe cites W. H. Auden's discussion of the sea as a place where "decisive events, the moments of eternal choice . . . occur." This passage from Auden's *The Enchafed Flood* is quoted in "Romantic Imagery," in *The Awakening,* Margaret Culley, ed., p. 202.

6. See William James, *The Varieties of Religious Experience: A Study in Human Nature* (New York: Collier Books, 1961), pp. 299-300.

7. Suzanne Wolkenfeld, "Edna's Suicide: The Problem of the One and the Many," *The Awakening*, Culley, ed., pp. 218-24, has categorized the critics' responses: Per Seyerstad and Kenneth Eble view Edna's suicide as a triumph; Donald S. Rankin, George M. Spangler, and Cynthia Griffin Wolff see it as a defeat; Kenneth M. Rosen, Ruth Sullivan, and Stewart Smith view Chopin's attitude toward Edna's death as purposefully ambiguous. The views of Rankin, Eble, Seyerstad, Spangler, and Wolff are reprinted in *The Awakening*.

8. Per Seyerstad, *Kate Chopin: A Critical Biography* (Oslo and Baton Rouge: Universitets forlaget and Louisiana State University Press, 1969), pp. 194, 160.

9. Sisterhood with other women, which is notably lacking in Chopin's novel, gives many women today a strength they would not have alone.

10. For similar expressions of dissatisfaction with suicide as the conclusion to the story of the feminist heroine, see Patricia Meyer Spacks, *The Female Imagination* (New York: Knopf, 1975), pp. 75-77, 147-150; and Elaine Showalter, *A Literature of Their Own* (Princeton: Princeton University Press, 1977), pp. 276-80.

## CHAPTER 4.    REFUSING TO BE VICTIM: MARGARET ATWOOD

1. Page numbers refer to quotes from the Simon and Schuster edition of *Surfacing*, 1972.

2. In "A Reply," *Signs* 2, 2 (Winter 1976), pp. 340-341, Atwood has noted that American critics (many of them female) have focused attention on the woman as victim, as I will do, while Canadian critics have viewed the woman as a metaphor for

Canada. Atwood herself is keenly interested in Canadian national identity, as her book *Survival: A Thematic Guide to Canadian Literature* (Toronto: Anansi Press, 1972) makes clear, as well as in female identity. However, she has noted that "the positions are the same whether you are a victimized country, a victimized minority group or a victimized individual," *Survival,* p. 36.

3.  Some of the men in powerboats are Canadians, as she later learns.

4.  In a letter to Dan Noel dated December 14, 1974, Atwood stated that "what is *actually* seen during the diving scene is the father's corpse."

5.  See M. Esther Harding, *Women's Mysteries: Ancient and Modern* (New York: Bantam Books, 1973), especially pp. 138–49.

6.  Barbara Hill Rigney, *Madness and Sexual Politics in the Feminist Novel: Studies in Brontë, Woolf, Lessing, and Atwood* (Madison: University of Wisconsin Press), p. 111.

7.  Adrienne Rich, *Of Woman Born* (New York: Bantam Books, 1977), p. 245.

8.  Letter from Canadian critic William C. James to Carol P. Christ, dated May 13, 1979. See his "Atwood's *Surfacing:* The Alternatives Transcended," forthcoming in *Canadian Literature.*

9.  "Margaret Atwood: Beyond Victimhood," *American Poetry Review* 2, 6 (November-December 1973), p. 44. A similar narrow political definition of feminism seems to underlie Susan Fromberg Schaeffer's statement that *Surfacing* is not concerned with "liberationism," in "It Is Time That Separates Us: Margaret Atwood's *Surfacing,*" *Centennial Review* 18, 4 (Fall 1974), p. 319.

10. See Ruth M. Underhill, *Red Man's Religion* (Chicago: University of Chicago Press, 1972); Rita Gross, "Exclusion and Participation in Aboriginal Australian Religion" (Ph.D. dissertation, University of Chicago, 1974); and Mircea Eliade, *The Sacred and the Profane* (New York: Harcourt, Brace & World, 1959), ch. 3, esp. pp. 138–47.

11. See Rosemary Ruether, *New Woman/New Earth: Sexist Ideologies and Human Liberation* (New York: Seabury Press, 1976), esp. ch. 1.

12. See Rita M. Gross, "Menstruation and Childbirth as Ritual and Religious Experience in the Religion of Australian Aborigines," *Journal of the American Academy of Religion* 45, 4 (December 1977), Supplement, pp. 1147–1181; and Penelope Washbourn, *Becoming Woman: The Quest for Wholeness in Female Experience* (New York: Harper & Row, 1977); and *Seasons of Woman: Song, Poetry, Ritual, Prayer, Myth, Story* (New York: Harper & Row, 1979).

13. Rosemary Ruether, "Motherearth and the Megamachine," in *Womanspirit Rising,* Carol P. Christ and Judith Plaskow, eds. (New York: Harper & Row, 1979), p. 51.

## CHAPTER 5.  FROM MOTHERHOOD TO PROPHECY: DORIS LESSING

1. The following abbreviations are used for the novels in the *Children of Violence: Martha Quest, MQ; A Proper Marriage, PM; A Ripple from the Storm, RS; Landlocked, L; The Four-Gated City, FGC.* Page numbers from the first four volumes refer to the New American Library Plume Book editions, New York, 1970 (original publication dates, 1952, 1954, 1958, 1965). Page numbers in the final volume refer to *The Four-Gated City* (New York: Bantam Books, 1970). Page references appear in the text.

2. See Florence Howe, "A Conversation with Doris Lessing" (1966), *Contemporary Literature* 14, 4 (Autumn 1973).

3. Quoted in Doris Lessing, "What Looks Like an Egg and Is an Egg?" *New York Times Book Review,* May 7, 1972, p. 42.

4. Michael Novak, *The Experience of Nothingness* (New York: Harper & Row, 1970), p. 115.

5. Barbara Hill Rigney, *Madness and Sexual Politics in the Feminist Novel: Studies in Brontë, Woolf, Lessing, and Atwood* (Madison: University of Wisconsin Press, 1978), p. 88.

6.  The relation between mother and daugher is more strained than that between father and son, because when a son rejects his father as a role model, there are many cultural and literary heroes to emulate. But when a woman rejects her mother, there are no other images to choose. Thus there rarely can be a clean break between mother and daughter, nor is a situation of neutrality often possible. For recent discussions of the mother-daughter relationship, see Adrienne Rich, *Of Woman Born* (New York: Bantam Books, 1977), pp. 218-259; and Nancy Friday, *My Mother/My Self: The Daughter's Search for Identity* (New York: Delacorte Press, 1977); for a study of the mother-daughter relation in Lessing, see Ellen I. Rosen, "Martha's 'Quest' in *Children of Violence,*" *Frontiers* 3, 2 (Summer 1978), pp. 54-59.

7.  Sydney Janet Kaplan, "The Limits of Consciousness in the Novels of Doris Lessing," *Contemporary Literature* 14, 4 (Autumn 1973), pp. 536-49.

8.  Lessing believes that what psychiatrists often label madness is really an acute sensitivity to the chaos in the family and society. For discussions of Lessing's views of therapy, madness, and sanity in relation to the views of R. D. Laing, see Barbara Hill Rigney, *Madness and Sexual Politics in the Feminist Novel,* pp. 1-12, 65-90; and Marion Vlastos, "Doris Lessing and R. D. Laing: Psychopolitics and Prophecy," *Proceedings of the Modern Language Association* 91, 2 (March 1976), pp. 245-58.

9.  This phrase was used by a student in my course at Wesleyan, Anne Murphy, in an essay titled "A Woman's Book," unpublished.

10. Privately printed for the C. G. Jung Institute, Zurich, July 1956, quoted in Ann Belford Ulanov, *The Feminine in Jungian Psychology and Christian Theology* (Evanston: Northwestern University Press, 1971), pp. 207-10.

11. See Nancy Shields Hardin, "Doris Lessing and the Sufi Way," *Contemporary Literature* 14, 4 (Autumn 1973), pp. 565-81.

## CHAPTER 6.    HOMESICK FOR A WOMAN, FOR
OURSELVES: ADRIENNE RICH

1.  Barbara Charlesworth Gelpi and Albert Gelpi, "Introduction,"
    *Adrienne Rich's Poetry: Texts of the Poems, the Poet on Her
    Work, Reviews and Criticism* (New York: Norton, 1975), p. xi.

2.  Adrienne Rich, *Diving into the Wreck* (New York: Norton,
    1973). Page references to poems from *Diving into the Wreck*
    appear in parentheses in the text preceded by *DW*.

3.  See, for example, Albert Gelpi, "On Adrienne Rich: The Poetics
    of Change," pp. 130–48, and Robert Boyers, "On Adrienne
    Rich: Intelligence and Will," pp. 148-60, in *Adrienne Rich's
    Poetry*, for negative views of Rich's politics.
    See Erica Jong, "Visionary Anger," pp. 171-75; and Wendy
    Martin, "From Patriarchy to the Female Principle: A Chrono-
    logical Reading of Adrienne Rich's Poems," pp. 175-89,
    *Adrienne Rich's Poetry*, for positive views.

4.  Boyers finds this tendency of hers upsetting.

5.  The revelation of the androgyne in *Diving into the Wreck* (1972)
    parallels Rich's friend Mary Daly's vision of androgyny as the
    new being in *Beyond God the Father*. In "The Stranger," Rich
    describes herself as the "androgyne," "the living mind you fail
    to describe / in your dead language / the lost noun, the verb
    surviving / only in the infinitive" (19). Mary Daly expresses
    precisely the same ideas in similar language, suggesting mutual
    influence.

6.  Adrienne Rich, *The Dream of a Common Language* (New York:
    Norton, 1978). Page numbers appear in the text preceded by
    *DCL*.

7.  Adrienne Rich, *Of Woman Born: Motherhood as Experience
    and Institution* (New York: Bantam Books, 1977), p. 246.

8.  P. 226.

9.  An ironic sequel to Erich Neumann's book of the same title,
    which dealt solely with the origins and history of *male* con-
    sciousness.

10. While sharing Rich's admiration for the discipline and daring of these women, I am not convinced that women need to demonstrate their strength by following men in the "sport" of climbing the highest mountains "because they are there." The desire to "conquer nature" and "risk death" that inspires mountain climbers has always seemed to me to reflect a male bravado not unrelated to the will to dominate and lack of respect for life that Rich elsewhere identifies with a patriarchal sensibility. But see Charlotte Mills, "Why Women Climb Mountains," *WomanSpirit* 1, 2 (Winter, 1974), pp. 5-8, 15, for an alternative view.

11. See Chapter 6, "Hands of Flesh, Hands of Iron," pp. 117-48.

12. The images of the moon, which Rich views elsewhere as a symbol of the matriarchal spirit, and of ancient Stonehenge, recall ancient times when rituals and religion may have been created by women. I am not saying that Stonehenge necessarily was the site of woman-centered worship; only that Rich, like many other women, sees it as possibly having been such. See *Of Woman Born,* Chapter 3, "The Primacy of the Mother," pp. 70-97; and "Jane Eyre: The Temptations of a Motherless Woman (1973)," in *On Lies, Secrets, and Silence: Selected Prose 1966-1978* (New York: Norton, 1979), pp. 101-2, where Rich discusses the moon as "symbol of the matriarchal spirit."

13. See Zsuzsanna E. Budapest, *The Feminist Book of Lights and Shadows* (Los Angeles: Luna Press, 1976), Chapter 13; "Divination," pp. 110-25; and Sally Gearhart with Susan Rennie, *The Feminist Tarot: A Guide to Intrapersonal Communication* (Boston: Persephone Press, 1977).

14. Budapest, p. 120.

15. Budapest, p. 118.

16. Budapest, p. 116.

CHAPTER 7.     "i found god in myself . . . & i loved her
               fiercely": NTOZAKE SHANGE

1.  I refer to Black women simply as "women" in many places
    in this essay. Alice Walker's statement, "It is, apparently, in-
    convenient, if not downright mind straining for white women
    scholars to think of black women *as women,* perhaps because
    'woman' (like 'man' among white males) is a name they are
    claiming for themselves, and themselves alone" (*"One* Child
    of One's Own," by Alice Walker, *Ms.,* August 1978, 73), in an
    essay published just as this book was nearing completion, con-
    firmed my feeling that it is important to affirm that not all of
    a Black woman's experience is unique to her ethnic background,
    but that Black women because they are women share many
    experiences with women of other colors.

2.  Untitled introduction to *for colored girls who have considered
    suicide/when the rainbow is enuf* (New York: Macmillan,
    1976). Page references for all quotes from *for colored girls*
    will be cited in the text. In discussing the poems I will follow
    the order in the Macmillan edition, which is different from the
    order followed on the Original Cast album and in some pro-
    ductions of the play.

3.  Ntozake Shange, *For Colored Girls Who Have Considered
    Suicide/When the Rainbow Is Enuf* (Original Broadway Cast
    recording) (New York: Buddha Records, 1976), jacket notes.

4.  In this chapter, single slashes (/) are Shange's method of marking
    pauses, while double slashes (//) indicate the end lines of poetry;
    there are no double slashes in Shange's text.

5.  See Virginia Woolf, *A Room of One's Own* (New York: Harcourt
    Brace Jovanovich, 1957), p. 79; also see Josephine Donovan,
    "Feminist Style Criticism," in *Fiction* (Bowling Green, Ohio:
    Bowling Green University Popular Press, 1972), pp. 341–54; also
    Julia Penelope Stanley and Susan J. Wolfe (Robbins), "Toward a
    Feminist Aesthetic," *Chrysalis* 6, pp. 57–71.

6.  See Ntozake Shange, "takin a solo / a poetic possibility / a poetic
    imperative," *Nappy edges* (New York: St. Martin's Press, 1978),

pp. 2-12. See also her poem "i live in music," in the same work, pp. 126-27.

7. *Nappy edges,* p. 13.

8. *Nappy edges,* p. 16.

9. See Joyce A. Ladner, *Tomorrow's Tomorrow: The Black Woman* (New York: Doubleday, 1972), pp. 133-38.

10. *For Colored Girls* (Original Broadway Cast recording), jacket notes. This experience may be more typical of Shange's middle-class childhood than of a lower-class Black girl's childhood; and Ladner, who writes that "the standard conception of the 'protected, carefree, and non-responsible' child has never been possible for the majority of Black children," p. 57.

11. See Dianne Herman, "The Rape Culture," Jo Freeman, ed., *Women: A Feminist Perspective* (Palo Alto: Mayfield Publishing Co., 1975), pp. 41-63. Also see Susan Brownmiller, *Against Our Will: Men, Women, and Rape* (New York: Simon & Schuster, 1975), and Susan Griffin, *Rape: A Question of Consciousness* (New York: Harper & Row, 1979).

12. See Hallie Iglehart, "Unnatural Divorce of Spirituality and Politics," *Quest* 4, 3 (Summer 1978), pp. 20-22, for a discussion of the emergence of healing rituals in women's spirituality.

13. Shange, *For Colored Girls* (Original Broadway Cast recording), p. 28, line 7.

## CHAPTER 8.   TOWARD WHOLENESS: A VISION OF WOMEN'S CULTURE

1. Women's culture is a term used by women to describe cultural forms, including literature, art, music, dance, and ritual, which are created by women and reflect a female point of view.

2. *I Know You Know* (Los Angeles: Olivia Records, 1974), lyrics by Meg Christian, Thumbelina Music.

3. *The Changer and the Changed* (Los Angeles: Olivia Records, 1975), lyrics by Cris Williamson, Bird Ankles Music, BMI.

4.  *The Changer and the Changed,* lyrics by Cris Williamson, Bird Ankles Music.

5.  *A Live Album* (Ukiah, California: Redwood Records, 1974), lyrics by Holly Near, Hereford Music.

6.  *The Changer and the Changed,* lyrics by Cris Williamson.

7.  Kay Gardner, "Reflections on Spirituality and Women's Music," *Lady Unique* 1 (Autumn 1976), p. 26.

8.  *You Can Know All I Am: (A Collection of Short Plays)* (Ukiah, California: Redwood Records, 1976), lyrics by Holly Near, Hereford Music.

9.  *A Live Album,* lyrics by Jeffrey Langley and Holly Near.

10. *Imagine My Surprise! An Album of Songs about Women's Lives* (Ukiah, California: Redwood Records, 1978), lyrics by Holly Near, Hereford Music.

11. *The Changer and the Changed,* lyrics by Cris Williamson, Bird Ankles Music.

12. Gardner, "Reflections on Spirituality and Women's Music," *Lady Unique* 1 (Autumn 1976), p. 27.

13. Judy Chicago, *Through the Flower: My Struggle as a Woman Artist* (New York: Doubleday, 1975), p. 55.

14. *Through the Flower,* p. 56.

15. *The Dinner Party: A Symbol of Our Heritage* (Garden City, New York: Anchor Press/Doubleday, 1979), written and illustrated by Judy Chicago, designed by Sheila Levrant de Bretteville. *The Dinner Party* was exhibited at the San Francisco Museum of Modern Art, March 16–June 17, 1979.

16. *Through the Flower,* p. 55.

17. "Speaking for Myself," *Lady Unique* 1 (Autumn 1976), p. 55.

18. Mary Beth Edelson, "Mary Beth Edelson (commenting on her works)," in "Women's Survival Catalogue: Women's Spirituality," by Linda Palumbo, Maurine Renville, Charlene Spretnak, and Terry Wolverton, *Chrysalis* 6, p. 93.

19. Mary Beth Edelson, "Pilgrimage/See for Yourself: A Journey to a Neolithic Goddess Cave, 1977," *Heresies: A Feminist Journal on Art and Politics* (Spring 1978), pp. 96-99.

20.   Lucy Lippard, "Quite Contrary: Body, Nature and Ritual in Women's Art," *Chrysalis* 2, p. 32.

21.   Lippard, p. 35.

22.   See Gloria Feman Orenstein, "The Reemergence of the Archetype of the Great Goddess in Art by Contemporary Women," *Heresies* (Spring 1978), p. 80.

23.   For subscription information, write Box 263, Wolf Creek, Oregon 97497.

24.   Jean Mountaingrove, "Explorations in the Grove," *WomanSpirit* 1, 1 (Fall 1974), p. 7.

25.   Chellis Glendinning, "Lunation," *WomanSpirit* 3, 10 (Winter 1976), p. 23.

26.   Iglehart (and Pelikan), "Psychic Self-Defense: The Power of Free Women—An Incident at the Festival," *WomanSpirit* 2, 5 (Fall 1975), p. 42.

27.   Hallie Iglehart, "How the Festival Changed My Life," *WomanSpirit* 2, 5 (Fall 1975), p. 24.

28.   Kay Turner, "Contemporary Feminist Rituals" *Heresies* (Spring 1978), p. 21.

29.   Kay Turner, "Contemporary Feminist Rituals," p. 22.

30.   Kay Turner, "A Ritual Celebration," *WomanSpirit* 2, 5 (Fall 1975), p. 27.

31.   Kay Turner, "A Ritual Celebration," p. 25.

32.   See Carol P. Christ, "Why Women Need the Goddess," in *Womanspirit Rising, A Feminist Reader on Religion,* Carol P. Christ and Judith Plaskow, eds., pp. 273-87. The recent feminist books on the Goddess include Zsuzsanna E. Budapest, *The Feminist Book of Lights and Shadows* (Los Angeles: Luna Press, 1976), and *The Holy Book of Women's Mysteries* (Los Angeles: Luna Press, 1979); Anne Kent Rush, *Moon, Moon* (New York and Berkeley: Moon Books and Random House, 1976); Merlin Stone, *When God Was a Woman* (New York: Dial Press, 1976); Charlene Spretnak, *Lost Goddesses of Early Greece: A Collection of Pre-Hellenic Myths* (Boston: Beacon Press, 1984); Mary Daly, *Gyn/Ecology: The Metaethics of Radical Feminism* (Boston: Beacon Press, 1978); Naomi R. Goldenberg, *Changing of the Gods*

(Boston: Beacon Press, 1979); and Starhawk, *The Spiral Dance* (New York: Harper & Row, 1979). The Spring 1978 issue of *Heresies* was devoted to "The Great Goddess," and *Lady Unique* and *WomanSpirit* regularly publish articles on Goddesses.

33.   Judith Plaskow, "On Carol Christ on Margaret Atwood: Some Theological Reflections," *Signs* 2, 2 (Winter 1976), p. 337. Lucy Lippard, "Quite Contrary," p. 33.

35.   Lippard, p. 33.

36.   Thealogy, a term coined by Naomi Goldenberg to refer to reflection on the meaning of Goddess, is the feminist equivalent of theology, which means reflection on the meaning of God.

37.   Recent articles on the political implications of women's spirituality include Sally Gearhart, "Womanpower: Energy Resourcement," *WomanSpirit* 3, 9 (Summer 1976), pp. 19-23; Hallie Iglehart, "Unnatural Divorce of Spirituality and Politics," *Quest* 4, 3 (Summer 1978), pp. 12-24; "Hypatia's Column: The Politics of Women's Spirituality" (3 views), Gloria Z. Greenfield, Judith Antares, and Charlene Spretnak, *Chrysalis* 6 (November 1978), pp. 9-15.


## AFTERWORD TO THE THIRD EDITION


1.   Carol P. Christ, *Odyssey with the Goddess: A Spiritual Quest in Crete* (New York: Continuum, 1995).

2.   Carol P. Christ, *Laughter of Aphrodite: Reflections on a Journey to the Goddess* (San Francisco: Harper and Row, 1987).

3.   This essay "Rethinking Theology and Nature" is printed in Judith Plaskow and Carol P. Christ, eds. *Weaving the Visions: New Patterns in Feminist Spirituality* (San Francisco: Harper and Row, 1989), pp. 314-325.

4.   See "Learning from My Mother Dying" in Christine Downing, ed., *The Long Journey Home: Revisioning the Myth of Demeter and Persephone for Our Time* (Boston: Shambhala, 1994), pp.

125-131; also in Carol P. Christ, *Odyssey with the Goddess: A Spiritual Quest in Crete* (New York: Continuum, 1995), "Death," and "Grief," pp. 18-26.

5.  A command to tell his story again and again until he understood it was given to the protagonist of Elie Wiesel's *The Gates of the Forest*, trans. Frances Frenaye (New York: Avon Books, 1967). Reading this book led me to write my dissertation on the work of Elie Wiesel.

6.  See Christine Downing, *The Goddess* (New York: Crossroad, 1981), *Journey through Menopause* (New York: Crossroad, 1987), and *Women's Mysteries* (New York: Crossroad, 1992); Karen McCarthy Brown, *Mama Lola* (Berkeley: University of California Press, 1991); Starhawk, *The Fifth Sacred Thing* (New York: Bantam Books, 1993); Mary Daly, *Outercourse* (San Francisco: HarperSanFrancisco, 1992); and Clarissa Pinkola Estes, *Women Who Run with the Wolves* (New York: Ballantine, 1992).

7.  Sue Monk Kidd, *Ariadne's Thread* #1 (February 2, 1995), p. 4.

# Index

161

*is enuf* (Shange), xxx–xxxi, 6,
    97–117
*Four-Gated City, The* (Lessing),
    xxv, xxviii, 59–73
Freud, Sigmund, 139

### G

Gardner, Kay, 122, 123
Glendinning, Chellis, 126
"Goddess," celebration of, 47, 91,
    108, 117, 124–125, 128,
    150–151
Goldenberg, Naomi, 12
*Golden Notebook, The* (Lessing), 8
Griffin, Susan, 22

### H

Healing rituals, 116, 117, 121, 122,
    126–129
*Hero with a Thousand Faces, The*
    (Campbell), 9
Hicks, Margaret, 125
Hierarchical mentality, opposition
    to, 25–26, 101–102

### I

Identity, self, importance of in spir-
    itual quest, 31, 59–60, 67, 69,
    70–72. *See also* Self-image
Iglehart, Hallie, 127
Innocence, female delusion of,
    43–44, 49, 58–59
Insanity, *see* Madness

### J

James, William, 20–21, 22

### K

Kahlo, Frieda, 125
Kaplan, Sydney Janet, 64

### L

Language, deformation of, xiii–xv
Language, women's creation of
    new, 1–12, 81, 83, 84–86, 95,
    101–102
Lesbianism, and new naming of
    self, 81–82, 83, 85, 89–95
Lessing, Doris, xxviii, xxix–xxx,
    1–2, 8, 10, 39, 55–73, 78, 101,
    116, 119
Levertov, Denise, xxix
Lippard, Lucy, 125–126, 129, 130
Loneliness, vs. solitude, 94. *See
    also* Solitude, women's

### M

Madness: confronting, 64–68, 144;
    and personal sense of worth, 16,
    100
Marriage, and search for self-
    awareness, 27–39. *See also*
    Relationships
*Martha Quest* (Lessing), 1–2,
    55–57
Marton, Ree, 125
*Memoirs of an Ex-Prom Queen*
    (Shulman), 8
Men, women seeking fulfillment
    through loving, 28–29, 33, 34,
    63–64, 77–78, 83–84, 105–106,
    108, 109–116. *See also* Rela-
    tionships
Mendieta, Anna, 125
Menstruation, women's feelings